COLLECTING

Blue Willow

Identification & Value Guide

M. A. Harman

COLLECTOR BOOKS
A Division of Schroeder Publishing Co., Inc.

The current values in this book should be used only as a guide. They are not intended to set prices, which can vary from one section of the country to another. Auction prices as well as dealer prices vary greatly and are affected by condition as well as demand. Neither the author nor the publisher assumes responsibility for any losses that might be incurred as a result of consulting this guide.

Searching for a Publisher?

We are always looking for people knowledgeable within their fields. If you feel that there is a real need for a book on your collectible subject and have a large comprehensive collection, contact Collector Books.

On the cover:
Royal Charger, $15.00 – 25.00, courtesy of Paul and Bonnie Houck;
Cow Creamer, $1,200.00+, courtesy of Jeanne Berlew;
Pitcher/Bowl Set, $750.00 – 950.00, courtesy of Pam Donahue.

Cover design by Beth Summers
Book design by Karen Smith

Collector Books
P.O. Box 3009
Paducah, Kentucky 42002-3009

www.collectorbooks.com

Copyright © 2001 by M. A. Harman

Contents

Dedication

Acknowledgments

This has been a wonderful experience for me. I would like to thank the Lord for the energy and strength to get through this project. I want to thank my husband for his undying devotion to me even when I was facing a deadline! He went above and beyond the call of duty, helping me research, going to the library, reading correspondence, and more. This book was no small chore for me, but a great achievement.

What makes this Willow collecting book so special is that I am a Willow collector. Many of my fellow Willow collectors were very excited to hear that a Willow collector was publishing a book. The response to my book was overwhelming. My main intent was to open it up to any collector who wanted to be a part of the project. Willow collectors from around the world responded, resulting in a wonderful sense of friendship.

To the following collectors who donated their photographs and sent me many e-mails about sizes and other information, thank you: Jackie Casey, Glenn and Rosemary Gibbs, Loren Zeller, Eileen Callow, Gary and Sandy Osenbaugh, Brenda Osmer, William and Vitalia Hodgetts, Jeanne Berlew, Irina Aladinski, and Paul Berklayd.

My heartfelt thanks goes out to Tim Allen, Connie Rogers, and Jeff Siptak. I appreciate their time spent proofreading my rough draft, responding to my countless e-mails, providing photographs, and supporting me. A special thanks to Jeff for the write-up in the *Willow Review*. Their kindness will never be forgotten.

Thanks to Pam Donahue, who opened her home up to me twice and allowed me to photograph her wonderful collection. For a Willow collector, I was in complete awe of the amount of Willow she owned. I didn't even notice she was wearing a Willow design dress! Anyone who knows Pam knows she has another love, her cats (one of which I have deemed as my photo assistant, Minnie).

Thanks to my mother and father, Paul and Bonnie Houck, my daughters, Amanda and Amber, my in-laws, David and Agnes Harman, my grandmother, Dolly Schroeder, my husband's grandparents, Margaret and David Harman, Sr., my heartfelt thanks for all their support and love. To my best friend, Teri, thanks for being there for me. And to her father, Irving "Itchy" Sommers for his photography tips; his advice was priceless and appreciated.

To the many members of IWC (International Willow Collectors) whose support and kind words got me through many days. And to anyone I forgot to mention, you are appreciated very much.

Introduction

I am a Willow collector at heart. My love of Willow began many years ago in my great-grandmother's kitchen. My great-grandmother stored my two unwed aunts' Blue Willow dinnerware sets in her kitchen. My two aunts purchased a piece each week until their sets were complete, from a local five-and-dime store called J.J. Newberry's. The Blue Willow dinnerware sets were made by Royal China Company. Sadly, my Aunt Mary passed away at an early age. My Aunt Rose never married, and passed away a few years ago. As a child I remember my mother washing their dishes and placing them carefully back in the cupboard. My mother inherited one of the sets, a service for 12 of Royal Blue Willow. She split the set into two settings for six, giving me one and keeping one for herself. My mother and I display our sets in our hutches, and remember my aunts each time we glance at them.

You can imagine my surprise when visiting my husband's grandmother's house for the first time and finding out she had collected Willow for over 50 years herself! Her home was full of Willow.

My love of Willow has grown over the years from an inherited fancy to a collection of which I am quite proud. My research is ongoing and I welcome hearing from you and seeing your finds. Feel free to e-mail me at: mharman@sunlink.net.

The purpose of this book is to illustrate, identify, and define the "sample" of Willow ware presented. As a collector of Willow ware I know what the ordinary collector wants in a book: an accurate, easy-to-follow book about something that's fun to collect.

LISTINGS

I have consulted many advanced Willow collectors on the best research books and formats. In this book I have complied a sampling of Willow and arranged the pieces in alphabetical order. I have indexed and cross-referenced the Willow items for ease in finding them.

This book is arranged in basic term "ABC" order for your convenience. There is no index for individual pieces since even the novice collector can thumb through the book and locate a cup or a bowl with ease. The Photo Gallery starts with "Ashtrays" and ends with "Wash Pitcher and Basin." Plates such as collector series and grill are generalized under "plates" as are "cups" (measuring, punch, etc.)

Please familiarize yourself with the book layout and the terms I use to describe Willow pieces. There are different terms that people like to use; one might call a pitcher and bowl set an ewer and basin. Neither is wrong; it's one's preference. In the glossary I have defined the terminology used in the photo captions. The Willow ware in this book is described with a standardized terminology used by many collectors.

PRICING

The prices were obtained based on these factors: demand, quality, rarity, manufacturer, desirability, origin, and condition. All prices listed are for pieces in excellent condition. Prices change due to supply and demand, region, condition, and age. No price guide can be 100% accurate. The prices were derived from comparing recent market values at antique shows, on the Internet, and at shops. The prices are only meant to be a guideline and may rise or fall for any number of reasons. Neither the persons credited with the photographs, the author, nor the publisher is responsible for any outcome from the use of the prices in this book. They are meant to be a guideline, not an appraisal. Consult your yellow pages for a reputable antique appraiser or, if available, a reputable Blue Willow dealer in your area for an estimated price for your item.

PHOTO CAPTIONS

When assembling the hundreds of photos I had collected over the years, I had the task of trying to explain each item to you, the reader. My goal was to include the size and company, when available, and a reference to the mark. You should be able to flip back easily to the marks section and find the number to which I referred. I included a brief description of the item when necessary and listed interesting features of the piece.

The photo captions include the plate number, item, size, manufacturer (if known), reference to mark number, brief description (if necessary), person donating the photo, and price range. Pattern is assumed to be traditional (standard) Willow unless otherwise noted.

If you see $ND, this means the piece is a one-of-a-kind, rare item, too unique to price.

INDEX

I have provided two types of indexes for your convenience: patterns and manufacturers. The manufacturers index is divided into American, English, Japanese, and other origins. After you read over the book once or twice you should get a feel for how I arranged the book and what terms I used.

THE WILLOW COLLECTOR

The Willow collector himself is a rare find; this normally reasonable person will lose all logic when it comes to collecting the ware he loves. We Willow collectors buy what we have no more room for, "investment pieces," knowing we are getting a deal, and we try to explain to others how we *need* to buy yet another piece. Once you start collecting you can't stop; you buy one piece then suddenly you are a die-hard Willow collector. You feel the need to have everything in Willow.

Then you start to notice that Willow comes in many forms: metals, ceramics, glass, paper, linens, jewelry, and more. Where do you start? You begin to research Willow, and you notice not only does it come in many different forms but it has many different manufacturers, comes from different origins, and has variant patterns and numerous color variations. What do you do now? First, decide what you like.

WHAT IS BEST FOR YOU?

My family collects Willow differently. I collect what I like (which is everything Willow), based on quality and price. I love Willow, but I do have a budget. My father-in-law collects according to quality, rarity, and price. He somehow always finds a great deal. My mother, on the other hand, normally only matches her pattern. Once she finds something that matches her pattern, the price doesn't matter, as long as it is in excellent condition. There is a wide range of Willow items to collect, so one never has every piece, and something different is always turning up.

Determine your likes and dislikes, as well as your budget. Collecting is fun and will be if you stay within your means. Once you decide what you are going to collect, whether it be one pattern or every pattern, you need to educate yourself on what is out there.

TIPS

Matching your pattern requires research. Find out who the maker is simply by turning over the item and seeing if there is a mark there. Please refer to the Marks section in the back of this book. There are also some very good reference books on manufacturers' marks listed in the bibliography. Sometimes these books can be costly, but they are well worth it when you are researching marks.

Early in my collecting years I found myself at an antique show looking at a piece in complete confusion. I knew I needed a missing lid or plate, but did it match? Here are a few tips that might help you when you are on the road.

Carry a small photo album of your collection. Try to find the kind that has the area on the bottom of the page where you can jot down notes.

In a hand-held notepad, jot down the mark and the size of the piece. For example, the teapot from which you are missing a lid. Normally you can measure the diameter of the opening.

It's a good idea to research the manufacturer that you are collecting. You can normally tell who manufactured your piece by simply flipping over the piece and looking at the mark on the back. The manufacturer's name may be on the mark. Or you might need to look into some good marks books, as I mentioned earlier. Often manufacturers produced a flyer that featured the complete lines that they designed.

RESEARCHING WILLOW

How do you determine exactly what kind of Willow you have? This is not an easy question when dealing with the many variations of Willow. It depends how particular you are as a collector. Some collectors research and catalog everything about their Willow, while others simply buy pieces and set them on a shelf. There is nothing wrong with either scenario. For those who do want to know more about their Willow, here is some advice. First, you can generally quickly determine what you have — a plate, bowl, cup, etc. If not, you can start by looking for the piece in various Blue Willow books that are on the market. You can generally find something similar to what you have. Once you figure out what the piece is, you will want to know who made it. Hopefully you can just flip over the item and see a manufacturer's mark on the bottom. However, a mark doesn't always make the manufacturer obvious. There are several really good reference books that you could find at your local library or purchase from a bookstore; these are listed in the bibliography.

PURCHASING WILLOW

I don't know if you're anything like I was when I first started collecting, but I didn't know much about Willow. I just knew I liked it and *had* to buy every piece I saw. Now I tend to favor rare pieces and am choosy about the condition of the pieces I buy. Here is some good advice that I wish someone had told me when I first starting collecting. First, educate yourself. Learn to identify the patterns, keep up to date with marks, and acquaint yourself with price guides. Familiarize yourself with the ranges that most antique books use to get an idea of what pieces are worth. I have often heard people say "I thought it was old Willow but when I asked around I found out it was newer." And that's fine if you purchase the Willow knowing it's new, but when you purchase it thinking it's older, you feel cheated.

You need to determine the value of the piece to know if you are getting a deal. Sometimes a piece will command more from the dealer because of its rarity. It really depends on what you are willing to pay for it and how badly you want that piece in your collection. Again, it's your preference. You should quickly get to know the price ranges for cups, saucers, plates, etc., noting that certain manufacturers dominate higher price ranges due to name and quality alone.

You will need to use your reference books, knowledge, and common sense when purchasing a piece of Willow. I personally like to pay no more than I know what the item is worth. I like a good deal; most collectors do. Occasionally I will overindulge on a piece that I really desire, knowing I am overpaying for it. But rarely do I overlook the condition of the piece. I normally do not purchase items that are considerably damaged.

Here are some tips when examining a piece of Willow. Pick up the piece carefully and check the overall appearance of the piece. Most collectors will notice chips and cracks. But what about crazing and spur marks? Crazing marks are the detailed cracks in the glaze caused by the uneven contraction of the glaze and body. Exposure to heat and/or moisture can cause crazing. Age can also play a part in crazing. Crazing is normally easy to catch just by looking at the piece. Depending on how bad the crazing is, it can sometimes appear brownish. Spur marks are small irregular areas on the piece left by the clay supports that stack and separate the pieces in the kiln in the firing stage.

Your sense of touch is an excellent source when checking for damage. Glide your fingertips over the entire surface; go over the edges and over the flat surface. Make sure you lift lids and study the inner rims and lid rims. Remember to check teapot spouts. Also note the overall glaze coverage. You may be able to see and/or feel any missed spots of glaze.

If you do spot an imperfection, you may want to bring it to the dealer's attention. If you are still willing to purchase the piece with the imperfection, maybe you can ask for a discounted price. Sometimes you win and sometimes you lose. I always ask for a discount no matter if it's mint or slightly damaged. It never hurts to try!

Asking questions and having knowledge are your only protections when purchasing Willow. If you see a piece you are unfamiliar with, it's understandable to be wary of buying it, especially if you're afraid it is a reproduction. Here are some simple questions when approaching a dealer (this is also true if you are purchasing off the Internet; ask questions before you buy/bid. It may save you some headaches in the long run): Does the seller know where the piece came from? Where did the seller get it? Estate sale? Yard sale? Does the seller know an estimated age? Any knowledge of the mark?

Just because a seller says it's old or rare doesn't mean it is. You really need to jot down the information and check on it yourself before making a big purchase. It's better to be safe than sorry. And if you are worried the piece will be sold while you're checking, some dealers will hold it for you for a small percentage. Most will gladly give the money back if you change your mind, but be sure to ask if you can get your money back if you decide not to purchase it. These are only tips, and ultimately you must make the decision.

REPRODUCTIONS VERSUS NEW WILLOW

My view on reproductions might not be shared by everyone. Manufacturers have the right to reproduce pieces, but they also have a responsibility to the buyer to clearly state that it is a reproduction. One may consider everything produced after the first Willow pattern a reproduction. A fellow collector once offered this simple definition: reproductions are generally considered by antique collectors to be usually poor quality replicas of pieces. Normally a reproduction will be inexpensive; that could be your first clue. Marks that are used on some reproductions are obvious imitations of marks from years past.

One that comes to mind is the lion and unicorn mark (see Mark 13 for example of authentic mark); buyers are easily confused by this mark, associating the newer mark with old marks. Pay attention to detail. Marks on reproductions often appear unclear, almost sloppy in design. The piece might feel overly light or heavy when compared to similar items. Also a good tip, look at the overall wear of the item.

Sometimes you can tell if you look at the bottom rim; note any wear? Take the time to look up the mark before jumping on a deal. If you buy reproductions and you're happy, that is fine. But be aware that new Willow items are making their way into the market at an increasing pace.

I was shopping one day with my daughter, when she pointed to a wall of plastic tea sets. She said, "Mom, look!" As most moms would, I glanced slowly, not getting excited, thinking I would see the newest toy out on the market. Then I saw it! My eyes widened with delight, a Blue Willow plastic toy tea set in a large box marked "Blue Willow" with the words "The pattern that has lasted for over 100 years." Two hundred years, I thought. There had to be over 20 sets on the wall. My first instinct was to buy them all. Then I took a breath and decided on two. They will probably end up in my attic and be discovered by my great-grandchildren. It was Willow, I had to have it. This was new Willow to me. It did not try to make itself out to be old; it was a whole new line of Willow to fit in with today's world. You may even be able to find new Willow in your local supermarket. This enables you to pick up new Willow to use everyday at a somewhat lower cost.

Some collectors, like me, do not use their older Willow. My husband's grandparents just recently stopped using their antique Blue Willow barrel shaped canister set. It was unsettling to me to hear the clinking of this valuable set each time they lifted the lids. I broke down and bought them a newer Willow canister set so they could put the other set away. This is why the newer Willow is great for those collectors who have to have Willow everywhere. If you are lucky you can find Willow in an array of new items: kitchenware, baking dishes, bathroom accessories, bedroom sets, children's sets, fabrics, and more.

Keep your eyes open; I had to do a double take when I was looking at kitchen curtains years ago at JC Penney. The curtains had several different plates on the bottom of the curtain. At closer examination I noticed the middle plate featured the traditional Blue Willow design. You will often find that artists love to use the Blue Willow design in their creations. Anne Geddes sometimes combines her adorable babies with Blue Willow teapots or cups and saucers. Keep your eyes open!

A Willow Legend

Many variations of the Blue Willow legend exist. This one at right appears on the back of a tin plate. Many collectors believe that salespersons hoping to sell Willow items created this legend. Legend or sales pitch? No matter where this Willow legend originated, any piece with its words is to this day highly collectible. There are shorter versions like the one here, and there are more extensive stories with the legend. This is just one example.

The Legend
Once upon a time there lived a very wealthy mandarin who had a beautiful daughter named Hong Shee. There was also a boy named Chang who loved Hong Shee. To keep them apart, the mandarin imprisoned his daughter in the palace. One day she escaped and the two lovers raced over the bridge to a waiting boat, her father in hot pursuit. They managed to elude the mandarin, reach the boat and sail away.
A storm developed, the boat foundered, and the couple was lost at sea. It is said two love birds appeared immediately thereafter – the spirits of Hong Shee and Chang.
Anon.

What is Willow?

Willow ware is often confused with other blue and white ware. Unknowingly people sometimes will call any blue and white patterns "Willow." The "traditional" Willow pattern will have these standard features: a willow tree in the center, leaning over a bridge, a tea house with three pillars forming a portico (columns), and a large orange tree behind the tea house. The bridge should have three figures crossing towards the island, and a boat should be on the lake with a man in it. Two birds flying towards each other are at the top center, and a fence crosses the foreground. A border will normally be present, but not always.

Does that mean if one or two of these components are missing that the piece you found isn't Willow? No.

Many Willow pieces lack certain components associated with the standard Willow pattern. For example, the Two Temples patterns generally do not have the birds, but these are Willow patterns. "A" Willow pattern is different from "the" Willow pattern. As a collector of Willow, I love to research what I have and classify the patterns. I don't suggest that you have to write down every pattern you have, but you should familiarize yourself with different Willow patterns.

Pieces displaying the traditional Willow pattern, which is over 200 years old, are highly collectible items. Many of the variations in the traditional Willow pattern are direct results of manufacturers creating their own versions of the Willow pattern. Burleigh, Turner, and Worcester are three manufacturers who did this.

Regardless of the variations found in the Willow pattern, one must have certain components of the "traditional" Willow pattern to state that it is Willow.

Familiarize yourself with the traditional Willow pattern, keeping in mind the basic components. There are many blue and white pieces that will be deemed Blue Willow ware; after researching, you will be able to make an educated decision when purchasing pieces for your collection.

Who determines what is Willow? The collector does. Some collectors are very open to variations of the Willow pattern, while others stick with the traditional pattern. Neither is wrong. Collect what you like, not what others think you should collect.

Learn the basic components of Willow. Then allow yourself to "find" the Willow pattern within. And most of all, have fun!

The Willow pattern has responded to the test of time, remaining ever so collectible and desirable to those who collect it. The blue and white oriental design, characteristic of the Willow pattern, has thrived almost 200 years after its first known creation.

Due to the vast amount of pottery companies and closeness in dates, it becomes very difficult to pinpoint an exact company or designer to acknowledge as the inventor of the Willow pattern.

There is no sure system one can use to determine the exact dating or designation of pieces. Many myths have developed over the years, such as how many oranges are on the tree, the number of arches in the bridge, or how close the birds are to one another. One can only research and read opinions on how the Willow pattern originated.

Josiah S. Spode, a well-known Staffordshire potter, was said to have developed the "standard" Willow pattern from an original Chinese pattern called Mandarin. This was the original Willow design, and the only design which should be called the Willow pattern. Robert Copeland lists the standard features in his *Spode's Willow Pattern and Other Designs After the Chinese:* "the bridge with three persons crossing it, the willow tree, the boat, the main tea house, the two birds, and a fence in the foreground of the garden." Spode's first version of the Willow pattern was created around 1790, and his traditional pattern originated around 1810.

Around the 1790s other potters began designing the Willow pattern like the Wedgwood Company, whose successors would include William Adams & Sons, John Ridgway & Co., J & G Meakin, and Ashworth. Caughley, a pottery located in Shropshire, England, who employed such famous names as Thomas Turner and Thomas Minton, was also noted for its contributions to the Willow pattern.

From Josiah Spode's first version of the standard Willow pattern, Thomas Minton, working as a designer for Thomas Turner at Caughley, created the Mandarin pattern around the 1790s (Different researchers believe others should be designed with this pattern). The Mandarin pattern's features are quite similar to Spode's standard Willow pattern's. When comparing the standard Willow pattern to the Mandarin pattern, you will see that some of the features have been moved around and a figure has been added. Regardless of these changes, the Mandarin pattern has lasted and is loved by many.

Despite the other potteries who designed Willow patterns around the same period, a vast majority of collectors credit Spode as the creator of the traditional Willow pattern. Note the different techniques he used, such as the early works of 1790 being engraved all by line, except the round oranges on the trees. During the same time period the line work became finer in quality. Soon, with more experimenting, "stipple" punchwork took over much of the Willow pattern, creating what we know today as the standard Willow pattern.

After researching, one can come to the conclusion that Spode was indeed the creator of the standard Willow pattern. One thing is for sure, his pattern was popular; by 1830 approximately 200 pottery companies in England alone were manufacturing the Willow pattern.

From the first standard Willow pattern, many more versions developed. Thanks to manufacturers' creative touches and wanting to be individuals in a crowded market, there are many variations. The Willow pattern has survived being duplicated over and over again, in many forms and fashions. This seasoned masterpiece is one of the most sought out and loved patterns, passed down through generations to grace our dinner tables and china closets. The Willow pattern has stood the test of time, and will be around for a very long time to come.

The Blue Willow pattern is an intriguing area of interest for collectors. Classification of Willow patterns has been studied and researched by advanced Willow collectors for years. To this day we are still finding slight variations in these patterns. As you become more acquainted with the many patterns in Willow you will find that it is a good idea to familiarize yourself with the basic fundamentals that make up the traditional Willow pattern, the most common pattern that manufacturers used. Some manufacturers took the traditional Willow pattern and ever so slightly changed it to trademark their own Willow. You will soon learn the eye-catching differences that will help you identify certain manufacturers. The best way to acquire this talent is to research Willow publications. Refer to the bibliography for the reference books I used.

The terms I use to describe the center patterns and borders are common terms that should be part of a Willow collector's vocabulary. With any pattern there can be slight variations. Manufacturers sometimes did that purposely to give their Willow patterns a personal touch. Some of these pattern variations were created to be recognized for their designers. The list of patterns in this book does not include all the Willow patterns. You will learn that when you collect Willow it is perpetually fascinating because of the large array of pieces to find and collect.

In addition to the many manufacturers of Willow, there are many different colors to collect, from the traditional shades of blue to multicolored items. The list seems endless. Just when you think you have them all, up pops another piece. The variants, which I have included in the center patterns, are pertinent to Willow collecting. The need to introduce these terms to collectors is due to the overwhelming number of Willow items found with a variation in the traditional Willow pattern. "Variation" is a term most Willow collectors use loosely to describe Willow out of the norm.

These terms were compiled mainly from Mary Frank Gaston's *Blue Willow*, Robert Copeland's *Spode's Willow Pattern*, and the author's own findings. Jennifer A. Lindbeck's *A Collector's Guide to Willow Ware* also has beautiful photographs that show the detail of each pattern and border.

For excellent, in-depth, chronicled classification of the Willow pattern, recommended reading is Robert Copeland's *Spode's Willow Pattern*, a must for the true Willow collector.

The following pages illustrate the main Willow patterns that can be found. There may be only slight differences found in the patterns. It may be helpful to go to the plate noted and actually pick out the individual features listed to acquaint yourself with each pattern.

I have included the Royal Winton Pekin pattern becaue most collectors accept this as a Willow pattern. This is a highly collectible pattern, loved by many. I also refer to the "traditional" Willow pattern as "standard" Willow. I have used "traditional" for those who are more used to that term. The reasoning behind the term "standard" is that there are standard components needed to make up the Willow pattern.

The word variant means modify, different, or miscellaneous, and the term is used to characterize the many versions that collectors find in traditional Willow. I will use the word variant throughout this book when referring to different versions of the Willow pattern.

The term "simplified" will be used to describe Willow patterns that were formulated with simple lines to create the Willow design. The borders that accompany this design are also normally of a simple design. See Plate 96 for an example.

As with the center patterns, variations of the border patterns are commonly seen. The most common borders found have variations. When no border is found on a piece it is said to be "borderless." Sometimes the manufacturer used a simple line or a splash of color around the edge; some call this a simplified border. I will state this in the photo captions when necessary.

Standard (traditional) Willow center pattern
Three figures crossing the bridge, the willow tree cascading over the bridge, the boat with a figure in it, the tea house with an orange/apple tree behind it, an island on the left, a fence across the foreground, two birds at the top of the pattern, normally centered, flying towards each other, developed by Spode Factory, c. 1810.

Standard (traditional) Willow
reversed center pattern
The pattern elements are the same as in the standard (traditional) Willow pattern, but the pattern appears to be reversed. Note the position of the Willow tree and temple; both appear on the right.

Two Temples I center pattern
Seemingly two temples that overlap generally on the left side of the pattern, fence in foreground, two figures on bridge, a figure in doorway, figure by rocks, the willow tree at the bottom of the pattern, below the bridge an island appears at the top instead of two birds. This pattern is more rare than Two Temples II. It normally features the Butterfly border. See Plate 356.

Two Temples II center pattern
Similar to Two Temples I except there are two figures on the bridge, one figure in the temple door, no figure by the rocks, and the willow tree across the bridge. This pattern is occasionally seen reversed. Borders will vary. c. 1817. See Plate 349.

Two Temples reversed center pattern
Similar to Two Temples I and Two Temples II except the temple is on the right side instead of the left side of the pattern; often simplified. See Plate 18.

Mandarin center pattern
One figure in the boat, no bridge, normally features the Dagger border.

Royal Winton "Pekin" center pattern
The Pekin pattern can be described as Willow motifs in multicolored backgrounds like ivory, black, shades of blue and red, and even turquoise. See Plate 188.

Turner center pattern
The bridge is in the lower left position of the pattern, with two figures on it, no birds, pagodas are to the right with an island to the left. John Turner of Staffordshire, c. 1810 – 1812, created this pattern. Normally seen with the Scroll and Flower border. See Plate 368.

Booths center pattern

Named after the Booth Company in England. Resembles the traditional pattern except there is no fence in the foreground. The Bow Knot border will be found with this pattern. Once a trademark of Booth was copied by Japanese companies such as Nihon Koshitsu Toki Company, other English companies made variations of this pattern.

Worcester center pattern

Named after the Royal Worcester Porcelain Co. variation of the Willow pattern. Features three figures, three boats, no orange tree, no willow tree, and has the Scroll and Flower border. See Plate 49.

Burleigh center pattern

Named after the Burgess & Leigh Co. variation of the Willow pattern. Features five figures, no orange tree, and a Scroll and Flower border. First produced in the 1920s, full production 1929. See Plate 435.

Traditional border pattern in blue
An array of geometrical designs such as wheels, circular designs, and other ornamental designs, normally with a "fish roe" (resembles fish eggs in a line) around the outside border; sometimes has an inner Bow Knot border with geometrical designs.

Traditional border pattern in brown

Butterfly border pattern in blue
Features "winged" antennae designs. The butterflies themselves have many variations and are accompanied by geometrical designs. The fish roe may also be found on the outer rim of this border.

Butterfly border pattern in brown

Bow Knot border pattern
Commonly found with the Booths pattern, a repeated sequence of bows resembling drawings, and evenly placed geometrical designs.

Dagger or Fleur-de-lis border pattern
Normally seen in combination with the Mandarin pattern. Seemingly spiked dagger design on the inside border of a lattice design border.

Floral border pattern
Repeated floral designs – See Plate 333 for one variation of this border.

Scroll and Flower border pattern
Elegant scrolling curves and floral patterns make up this border design. See Plate 532.

Pictorial border pattern
Small-scale Willow pattern designs are arranged normally, spaced evenly throughout the border design. Sometimes the small-scale design will be a storytelling sequence of the Willow legend. Small-scale also referred to as Medallions. See Plate 31.

A fellow collector in the IWC (International Willow Collectors) chat room once asked "Why are there so many variations in the Willow pattern?" When attempting to answer this question, many members found themselves defending their personal opinions of the Willow pattern, and what was acceptable. What is acceptable? My answer is always the same: collect what you like. But is there a limit to what is Willow and what is not Willow? The answer is yes, there is a limit to what can be classified as a Willow pattern or variation. Some collectors need to see the birds, others need to see the willow tree. After hundreds of hours of research and collecting Willow for many years, I feel you must have a combination of certain Willow components. You should be able to clearly see the basic components of the standard Willow pattern.

The other blue and white lines are not Willow ware, but rather Oriental landscape designs. They might look like Willow ware but they are not. For example, take a look at Plate 195. I included this for a very important reason, to show an example of a similar blue and white ware that might be considered Willow ware. This pattern is called the Net pattern, consisting of a lot of floral designs and four smaller landscapes that feature a temple or palace.

I wanted to include this piece to show the novice collector the variations in what one feels is Willow. You decide: is it Willow or not?

Another area of variations is in color. I am still amazed at the numerous colors I come across in the Willow pattern, from the traditional blue and white, ranging from pale to dark blue, to the individual colors, to the appealing multicolored pieces. There are different terms to describe the ways one achieves color in ceramics. From conferring with several advanced collectors I came to the conclusion that the term multicolored and polychrome are synonymous. I was told by one collector that polychrome was a term used by the English and that the word multicolored was a word used by Americans. The term "Gaudy" Willow was used by Buffalo Pottery to refer to multicolored pieces. Often Ridgway pieces are referred to as Gaudy. Multicolored Willow is a fun and sometimes rare find.

There are certainly varied techniques that manufacturers used to achieve a different look to their Willow. Collectors wanting to know more about the actual process of ceramics should consult a book on that subject. Robert Copeland's *Spode's Willow Pattern* is an extraordinary book for its detailed look at the step-by-step process of manufacturing and the end results of ceramics.

Assessing the Age of Willow Ware

Determining the age of Willow ware is not a small task for the novice collector; even the advanced collector sometimes ponders over the exact timeline that a piece was made. The mark is the best way to determine the manufacturer and the estimated age. The manufacturer's mark is not an exact date calculator but it does assist you when determining age. Unmarked items are identified by comparing them to others like it. One can also compare an unknown piece to others like it in books and reference guides. See the Marks section of this book. Other good marks reference books are also found in the bibliography. I would recommend purchasing at least one for your reference.

When dating your pieces by marks, normally found on the bottoms of your pieces, be sure to keep in mind this tip. Use a good reference book, such as Geoffrey Godden's *Encyclopaedia of British Pottery and Porcelain Marks*. Keep in mind that the manufacturer's mark is normally dated by a time period. Manufacturers used certain marks for years, then changed their marks slightly, perhaps to include new partners or new company names. Whatever the reason, do take that into consideration when dating your Willow. Just because your piece says, for example, Coalport, doesn't necessarily mean it's the Coalport c. 1891 – 1920. You need to learn the marks and their differences. The best way to achieve this is to start your own personal library of research books. You don't have to memorize everything but it is a good idea to acquaint yourself with various marks.

Japanese Willow is one of my passions, especially Moriyama. Willow items marked "Moriyama" have a drawing of flowers in a basket, then the words "Made in Occupied Japan." Most Willow collectors agree that Japanese Willow features cute pudgy birds rather than the somewhat delicately lean drawn birds on traditional Willow. This is normally a simple way to identify unmarked Japanese Willow. If you are lucky enough to find a paper label on the bottom of a Japanese piece you can see how easily it could be washed off. I have found paper labels on many items, and listed the name of the company on the label if available. If no paper label is found on the item I listed it as unmarked. Unfortunately, the items without a paper label are difficult to date.

In 1891 the McKinley Tariff Act required that the name of the country where the piece was manufactured be labeled on each piece. *Kovel's New Dictionary of Marks* lists Japan with a date of 1921. Still some pieces were marked with the word "Japan" before the act in 1891; this is not a reliable rule. The words "Made in Occupied Japan" often appear on items that were exported from Japan from 1945 to 1952 at the end of World War II when allied forces "occupied" Japan. It is often pondered whether these items are more valuable when compared to items marked "Made in Japan." Once again it depends on how much it is sought after. The word "Nippon," the Japanese word for Japan, sometimes appears in various manufacturers' marks. Nippon can date 1918 and 1921.

The Noritake company was first registered in 1904 as Nippon Gomei Kaisha. The name became Nippon Toki Kabushiki Toki in 1917. The Noritake mark appears with an "M" in a wreath and "hand painted" underneath, then the words "Made in Japan" appear, which dates an item to about 1911 and means it was found in the area of Nagoya, Japan. This mark normally appears in green, and the wording might not always read as stated. The "M" in the wreath mark is that of the Morimura Brothers, distributors with offices in New York until 1941. The tree crest mark is the crest of the Morimura family. The Noritake company produced delightful fine porcelain ware and they continue to do so.

Moriyama Pottery, founded in Mori-Machi, was a well-known Japanese pottery. Hidekichi Nakamura founded Moriyama Pottery in 1911. He discovered in 1909 that the soil around Mori-Machi was quite suitable for making pottery. There are presently pottery studios in and around Mori-Machi that bring traditional Moriyama pottery techniques into this century.

Due to many companies' records being destroyed during war times, many marks cannot be dated.

Dating American Willow might not be as complicated as Japanese Willow, but it is no small task. The three largest U.S. Willow manufacturers were Buffalo, Homer Laughlin, and Royal. Let's take a brief stroll through American Willow history. American Willow has offered an assembly of lovely Willow items over the years.

The first American-made Blue Willow came from Buffalo Pottery, built in 1901 in Buffalo, New York. The line of "old" Willow Ware from 1905 to 1915 introduced Americans to a traditional Willow pattern in semi-vitreous china. The words "First Old Willow Ware Manufactured in America" can be found on pieces dated 1905, announcing the company's pride in this accomplishment. The company then experimented with colors creating what collectors call "Gaudy Willow." An extremely beautiful variety of colors adds rarity and excitement when collecting Buffalo Willow. In 1940 the name was changed to Buffalo Pottery, Inc. In

1956 the name was changed again to Buffalo China, Inc. In the 1960s the name became Buffalo China, Inc., owned by Oneida Corporation. Buffalo Willow items are normally easily identified by marks.

The Homer Laughlin China Company produced dinnerware from the 1920s to the 1960s. The company's Willow line has various marks, as well as unmarked Willow items. The company had a standard dating system of a combination of letters and numbers. The letters and numbers stood for several things: the year, either a single number, one, or four digits, or the plant with either a letter or a number.

I would recommend a good book of marks such as *Kovels' Dictionary of Marks* for precise dating. Comparing the similarity of other marked Homer Laughlin pieces can help identify the unmarked Homer Laughlin pieces. Homer Laughlin did not mark their hollowware line. Hollowware includes dinnerware serving pieces such as bowls, casseroles, pitchers, creamers, and sugar bowls. The flatware, plates, platters, and such, are normally marked and dated. Homer Laughlin manufactured two lines of Willow, decal-decorated and transfer printed. There are a lot of variations in the Homer Laughlin Willow line. Some pieces have advertising on them, others have color variations.

The Royal China Company's (Sebring, Ohio) line of Willow was a standard dinnerware from the 1930s to the 1980s. The rubber-stamp pattern can be found with Royal in a box, with a crown on top, unmarked. Royal China, underglaze (with a willow tree) Blue Willow displays the transfer printed line with Willow ware by Royal, Sebring, Ohio, and Royal Ironstone. These items can be found in the traditional blue, pink, green, and brown. Once you become acquainted with Royal China Company Willow you should be able to note the differences between this line and Scio Pottery Company, for instance. Be careful not to confuse the two; remember the Scio Pottery Company has a coupe shape, a contemporary shape. Scio's shape does not have a rim, is flat across the center, and tends to turn up slightly at the edge. When comparing the two you can also definitely see a difference in quality. Scio Pottery sometimes looks lax. I highly recommend Connie Rogers' *Willow Ware Made in the U.S.A. Identification Guide*. Thanks to Rogers' extensive research and hard work, many pieces are easily identified.

Large portions of some of the loveliest Willow ware were made in England. English marks are easily identified due to the hard work of two gentlemen abroad. Geoffrey Godden compiled the most extensive amount of information on marks in his guide, *Encyclopaedia of British Pottery and Porcelain Marks*. Robert Copeland's *Spode Willow Pattern and Other Designs After the Chinese* is an intriguing stroll through the detailed history of the Willow pattern and its English manufacturers.

The Staffordshire Knot is a cord tied in the shape of a bow or "knot." Many potters in the Staffordshire area used this mark. This mark can contain the initials or words that identify the manufacturer.

The best tools to correctly identify English pieces are the marks and a reliable book of marks. The two books I mentioned above are accurate and reliable research books. All the English marks in this book coincide with the dates found in their books.

Photo Gallery

Plate 1
Ashtray, fish figure, unmarked, red Willow, Willow motifs, hand-painted, $25.00 – 35.00. *Courtesy of Pam S. Donahue.*

Plate 2
Ashtrays, fish figures, 3"h., 5"l., unmarked, Japanese, $25.00 – 35.00 each. *Courtesy of David R. Harman, Jr.*

Plate 3
Ashtrays, whale figures, 3"h., 5"l., unmarked, Japanese, $25.00 – 35.00 each. *Courtesy of Paul and Bonnie Houck.*

Plate 1

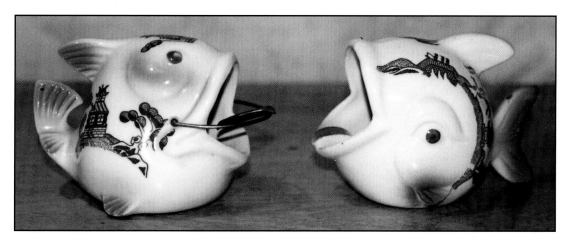

Plate 2

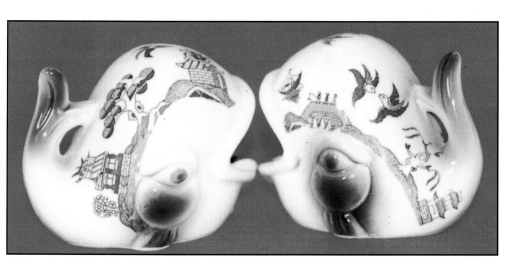

Plate 3

— *Photo Gallery* —

Plate 4
Ashtrays, left to right: 1¼"h., Crawford's Scotch Liqueur, James Green & Nephew Ltd., English, early 1900s; 5½"d., Ewell N.N. Stone & Co. Ltd., Mintons, c. 1912+; 2"h., 4¼"d., Usher's Scotch Whisky, James Green & Nephew Ltd., English, c. early 1900s. $135.00 – 150.00 each. *Courtesy of JWS.*

Plate 5
Ashtray, 3½"d., Thomas Cone Ltd., Royal Alma, Mandarin pattern, see Mark 15, $25.00 – 35.00. *Courtesy of Pam S. Donahue.*

Plate 6
Ashtray, 3½"d., Thomas Cone Ltd., Royal Alma, pink Willow, Mandarin pattern, see Mark 15, $25.00 – 35.00. *Courtesy of David R. Harman III.*

Plate 4

Plate 5

Plate 6

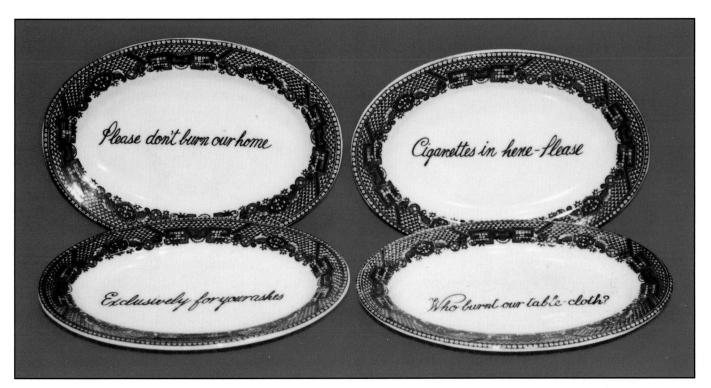

Plate 7

Plate 7
Ashtrays, 6"l, marked "JAPAN," traditional borders, see Mark 98, "Please don't burn our home," "Cigarettes in here – Please," "Exclusively for your ashes," and "Who burnt our table cloth?" $55.00 – 75.00 each. *Author's Collection.*

Plate 8
Bacon warmer, hot water plate, Booths, Tunstall, England, see Mark 11, Booths pattern, Bow Knot border, beautiful piece of Booths pottery; just like a hot water plate, there is a hole to pour hot water into, then the contents are placed onto the platter, covered with the lid, and placed on the table. Contents stayed warm due to the steaming water in the ceramic base. $250.00 – 525.00+. *Courtesy of Jackie Casey.*

Plate 8

Plate 9

Plate 11

Plate 10

Plate 9
Basket, 8"h. x 6"l., Spode c. 1800 – 1820, Two Temples I pattern, Butterfly border, possibly for bon bons, $800.00+. *Courtesy of Loren Zeller.*

Plate 10
Basket, 9"d., 7 ¾"h., unknown English mark covered by attached basket, $100.00 – 125.00. *Courtesy of David R. Harman, Jr.*

Plate 11
Batter Jug, 9½"h., Japanese, marked Moriyama, Made in Japan, see Mark 95, $125.00 – 150.00.

Plate 12
Batter jug/tray set, 9½"h., 6"l., marked Moriyama, Made in Japan, see Mark 95, $350.00 – 400.00 set. *Courtesy of Pam S. Donahue.*

Plate 13
Bedpan, unmarked, Staffordshire, English, rare, $1,200.00 – 1,500.00. *Courtesy of Jackie Casey.*

Plate 14
Bell, 8½"h., unmarked, $35.00 – 45.00. *Courtesy of Pam S. Donahue.*

Plate 12

Plate 13

Plate 14

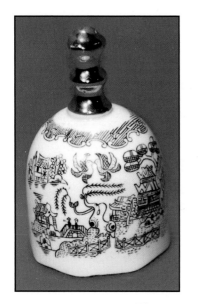

Plate 15

Plate 16

Plate 17

Plate 18

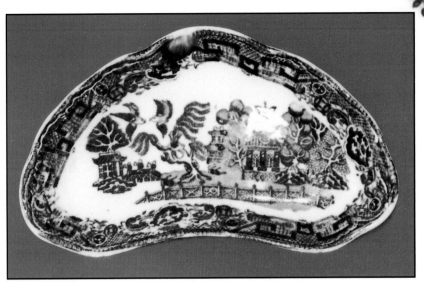

Plate 19

Plate 15
Bell, 4"h., unmarked, Imports Enesco Japan, red/gold paper label, $10.00 – 15.00. *Courtesy of Paul and Bonnie Houck.*

Plate 16
Bell, 4"h., unmarked, Imports Enesco Japan, red/gold paper label, $10.00 – 15.00. *Author's Collection.*

Plate 17
Biscuit jar, 7"h., unmarked, English, Minton, silver-plated lid and handle, $275.00 – 300.00. *Courtesy of David R. Harman, Jr.*

Plate 18
Left: biscuit jar, right: cookie jar, Moriyama, Japan; biscuit jar has a cane handle, tan accents, Two Temples II reversed pattern; cookie jar, standard (traditional) Willow pattern, see Mark 95, $150.00 – 175.00 each.

Plate 19
Bone dish, 6¼"l., Bourne & Leigh (E.B. & J.E.L. England mark), see Mark 13, $75.00 – 85.00. *Courtesy of David R. Harman, Jr.*

Plate 20
Bone dish, 6½", American, Buffalo mark, 1914, see Mark 105, $85.00 – 100.00. *Courtesy of David R. Harman, Jr.*

Plate 20

Plate 21

Plate 22

Plate 23

Plate 21
Bowl, 10¼"d., unmarked, English, oval shape, reticulated sides, scalloped rim, applied handles, used for holding chestnuts, commonly called a chestnut basket. $800.00+. *Courtesy of David R. Harman, Jr.*

Plate 22
Bowl, 11¼" handle to handle, 3½"h., unmarked, English, oval shape, reticulated sides, applied handles, chestnut basket or strawberry basket, beautiful example, $800.00+. *Courtesy of David R. Harman, Jr.*

Plate 23
Bowl, 9" x 7", 2¾"h., unmarked English, chestnut basket, example of the "Long Bridge" pattern, $850.00+. *Courtesy of Anne Backenstow, Hill Crest Antiques.*

— *Photo Gallery* —

Plate 24
Bowl, covered casserole, 10" handle to handle, 7½"h., marked Moriyama, Made in Japan, see Mark 95, possibly a bean pot, $125.00 – 150.00. *Courtesy of David R. Harman, Jr.*

Plate 25
Bowl, covered casserole, 9" handle to handle, 6 ½"h., marked Moriyama, Made in Japan, see Mark 95, possibly a bean pot, $125.00 – 150.00. *Courtesy of David R. Harman, Jr.*

Plate 26
Bowl, covered casserole, 9"d., Churchhill, England, see Mark 20, $55.00 – 75.00. *Courtesy of Gary and Sandy Osenbaugh.*

Plate 27
Bowl, 4¾"h., John Maddock & Sons Ltd., England, see Mark 44, instead of handles this bowl features two ladies' heads, interesting piece, $50.00 – 65.00. *Courtesy of David R. Harman, Jr.*

Plate 24

Plate 25

Plate 26

Plate 27

Plate 28

Plate 28
Bowl, 7"d., unmarked, with rubber stamped Two Temples II reversed pattern, two little birds in black, red flower design, black inner arrow border, $15.00 – 20.00. *Author's Collection.*

Plate 29
Bowl, 9"d., covered stackable vegetable, Moriyama, Made in Japan, see Mark 95, two shown, stacked set of four, "S" shaped sectional divide inside of bowl, $350.00+ for complete set of four. *Courtesy of David R. Harman, Jr.*

Plate 30
Bowl, 11¾"d., covered sectional dish, Moriyama, Made in Japan, see Mark 95, beautiful pattern inside each section, note two small holes on each handle, possibly for a cane handle, $175.00 – 200.00. *Courtesy of Brenda Osmer.*

Plate 29

Plate 30

Plate 31

Plate 32

Plate 33

Plate 34

Plate 31
Bowl, 10"w., 5"h., covered vegetable, marked Losal Center Willow, Keeling & Co. Ltd., and Burslem, Made in England, multicolored, lid features Pictorial border, $375.00 – 495.00. *Courtesy of William and Vitalia Hodgetts.*

Plate 32
Bowl, 9½" handle to handle, 6"h., covered vegetable, marked Societe Ceramique, Maestricht, Made in Holland, see Mark 136, $125.00. *Courtesy of David R. Harman, Jr.*

Plate 33
Bowl, 10¼" handle to handle, covered vegetable, unmarked, variant pattern known as "Ming" pattern, Booths, Tunstall, England, c. 1891+, Pictorial border with Willow legend in each scene, interesting flower bud finial, $100.00 – 125.00. *Courtesy of David R. Harman, Jr.*

Plate 34
Bowl, 5½"h., 11"l., covered vegetable, Gaudy by Ridgways, English, c. 1920s, beautiful cobalt blue finial and handles, $575.00 – 775.00. *Courtesy of JWS.*

Plate 35

Plate 36

Plate 35
Bowl, 7" x 6", covered vegetable, marked Wedgwood, England, in blue, imprinted with the numbers 12 08, $200.00 – 225.00. *Courtesy of Brenda Osmer.*

Plate 36
Bowl, 10" handle to handle, covered vegetable, round, unmarked, American, attributed to Homer Laughlin China Co., East Liverpool, Ohio, USA, $75.00. *Courtesy of Paul and Bonnie Houck.*

Plate 37
Bowl, 10" handle to handle, covered vegetable, green Willow, round, unmarked, attributed to Homer Laughlin China Co., East Liverpool, Ohio, USA, $75.00. *Courtesy of Pam S. Donahue.*

Plate 37

Plate 38

Plate 39

Plate 38
Bowl, 9¼" handle to handle, covered vegetable, square, Wood & Sons, Ltd. England, see Mark 75, $225.00 – 250.00. *Courtesy of David R. Harman, Jr.*

Plate 39
Bowl, 10" handle to handle, square covered vegetable, marked Ridgways, Bow/Quiver mark, see Mark 57, interior pattern, shown uncovered and covered, $225.00 – 250.00. *Courtesy of David R. Harman, Jr.*

Plate 39

Plate 40

Plate 40
Bowl, 10" handle to handle, round covered vegetable, marked Ridgways, Bow/Quiver mark, see Mark 57, $250.00 – 275.00. *Courtesy of David R. Harman, Jr.*

Plate 41
Bowls, left to right: 5¼"d., 6"d., and 7¼"d., mixing bowl set, Japanese, Karukon Ware, Two Temples II reversed pattern with birds, traditional border, $175.00 – 225.00.

Plate 42
Bowls, 7¾"d. and 9"d., nesting mixing bowls, set of three, Made in Japan, marked in black, $175.00 – 225.00. *Courtesy of David R. Harman, Jr.*

Plate 43
Bowl, 10½"d., mixing bowl, one in a set of three, Fiesta Kitchen Kraft by Homer Laughlin China Co., East Liverpool, Ohio, USA, marked Kitchen Kraft, 1930s, see Mark 116, "Chinese Willow Pattern," $125.00 – 150.00 for complete set, $50.00 large bowl. *Courtesy of Pam S. Donahue.*

Plate 41

Plate 42

Plate 43

Plate 44

Plate 45

Plate 44
Bowl, 3¼" h., Hazel Atlas Glass Company, Clarksburg, West Virginia, USA, see Mark 128, red Willow, half of the standard (traditional) Willow pattern on Moderntone Platonite glass, red trim on rim of bowl, $35.00 – 45.00. *Courtesy of Pam S. Donahue.*

Plate 45
Bowl, 5"d., cereal, Hazel Atlas Glass Company, Clarksburg, West Virginia, USA, see Mark 128, standard (traditional) Willow pattern on opaque white glass, no border, $10.00 – 12.00. *Author's Collection.*

Plate 46
Bowl, 4½"d., Jackson China Company, Falls Creek, Pennsylvania, USA, see Mark 113, red Willow, standard (traditional) Willow pattern, border is on interior of bowl, $12.00 – 14.00. *Courtesy of David R. Harman III.*

Plate 47
Bowl, 7¼"d., Mandarin Blue by Maurta, Japan see Mark 89, variant Willow pattern, $6.00 – 8.00.

Plate 46

Plate 47

Plate 48

Bowl, 5"d., Crown Staffordshire Porcelain Co. Ltd., Fenton, England, c. 1906+, see Mark 19, Chinese Willow pattern, $35.00 – 60.00. *Author's Collection.*

Plate 49

Bowl, footed, 11"d., 6½" h., Royal Worcester Porcelain Co. Ltd., Worcester, England; (Royal Worcester Spode Ltd.) see Mark 62, Worcester pattern, outer bowl, interior of bowl has silverplated rim and feet, $225.00 – 375.00+. *Courtesy of Glenn and Rosemary Gibbs.*

Plate 50

Bowl, 7"d., sauce or individual serving dish, one handled, marked semi–china, Ridgways, Bow/Quiver mark, see Mark 57, $30.00 – 35.00. *Courtesy of David R. Harman, Jr.*

Plate 51

Bowl, oval vegetable, unmarked, Japanese, red Willow, $15.00 – 20.00. *Courtesy of David R. Harman III.*

Plate 48

Plate 49

Plate 50

Plate 51

Plate 52

Plate 53

Plate 52
Bowl, vegetable, "R. Pilkington, Grapes Inn," unmarked, English, c. late nineteenth century, missing lid, $135.00 – 155.00. *Courtesy of JWS.*

Plate 53
Bowl, 9¾"d., 3¾"h., salad, unknown manufacturer, late 1990s, see Mark 139, traditional border inside and outside of bowl, standard (traditional) Willow pattern inside bowl, $50.00 – 75.00. *Courtesy of Paul and Bonnie Houck.*

Plate 54
Bowl, vegetable, Made in England, see Mark 42, $95.00 – 125.00. *Courtesy of David R. Harman, Jr.*

Plate 55
Bowl, vegetable, Charles Allerton & Sons, c. 1929 – 1942, see Mark 4, $110.00 – 150.00. *Courtesy of David R. Harman, Jr.*

Plate 54

Plate 55

Plate 56

Plate 57

Plate 58

Plate 58

Plate 58

Plate 56
Bowl, 9¼"d., 1¾"h., vegetable, William Adams & Sons, England, impressed with the numbers 7, 24, and 8, see Mark 3, $95.00 – 125.00. *Courtesy of David R. Harman, Jr.*

Plate 57
Bowl, 8"d., 2¼"h., vegetable, W.R. Midwinter, Ltd., see Mark 48, $95.00 – 125.00. *Courtesy of David R. Harman, Jr.*

Plate 58
Bowl, 9"d., 2½"h., vegetable, Barker Bros. Ltd., England, c. 1930 – 1937, see Mark 8, outside of bowl features a portion of the orange tree on one side while the other side has the two birds and a piece of the pattern design, $95.00 – 125.00. *Courtesy of David R. Harman, Jr.*

Plate 59
Bowl, 10"d., 2¾"h., vegetable, unmarked, English, $95.00 – 125.00. *Courtesy of David R. Harman, Jr.*

Plate 60
Bowl, 9"d., 2"h., vegetable, Charles Allerton & Sons, English, see Mark 4, outside of bowl features a piece of the pattern design with the section of the bridge and Willow tree on both sides, $110.00 – 150.00. *Courtesy of David R. Harman, Jr.*

Plate 61
Bowl, 10¼"d., 2½"h., pedestal vegetable, missing lid, unmarked, English, $150.00 – 175.00. *Courtesy of David R. Harman, Jr.*

Plate 59

Plate 60

Plate 61

Plate 62

Plate 63

Plate 64

Plate 65

Plate 62

Butter dish, 6"d. (in the wooden holder), 3¾"d. dish alone, unmarked, English, spreader, 5½" l., $175.00 for set. *Courtesy of David R. Harman, Jr.*

Plate 63

Butter dish, 6½"d. (in the wooden holder), unmarked, English, $85.00 – 100.00. *Courtesy of David R. Harman, Jr.*

Plate 64

Butter dish, 6"d. (in the wooden holder), unmarked, English, $85.00 – 100.00. *Courtesy of David R. Harman, Jr.*

Plate 65

Butter dish, 7"l., 3½"h. to knob, covered, unmarked, Japanese, holds ¼ lb. stick, $75.00 – 85.00. *Courtesy of David R. Harman, Jr.*

Plate 66

Butter dish, 9"d., 4"h., covered, Woods Ware & Sons, see Mark 75, red Willow, $155.00 – 165.00. *Courtesy of David R. Harman, Jr.*

Plate 67

Butter dish, 8"d., 3½"h., covered, unmarked, English, $125.00 – 145.00. *Author's Collection.*

Plate 68

Butter dish, 8"d., 4"h., covered, with insert, see Mark 42, Made in England, $155.00 – 165.00. *Courtesy of William and Vitalia Hodgetts.*

Plate 66

Plate 67

Plate 68

Plate 69

Butter dish, 7 ½"d., 3 ⅞"h., covered, three-piece covered set, with drain, J. Steventon & Sons, Ltd. England, c. 1923 – 1936, see Mark 65, $175.00 – 200.00. *Courtesy of Jeanne Berlew.*

Plate 70

Butter pats, left: 2½"d., Buffalo China Company, USA, see Mark 101, $25.00 – 45.00; right: 3"d., red Willow, no border, Jackson China Company, Falls Creek, Pennsylvania, USA, see Mark 113, $10.00 – 15.00. *Courtesy of David R. Harman III.*

Plate 69

Plate 70

Plate 71

Plate 72

Plate 73

Plate 71
Butter warmer, Japanese, unmarked, warmer sits on iron stand with a candleholder underneath with only a border on it, $100.00 – 125.00. *Courtesy of David R. Harman, Jr.*

Plate 72
Candleholders, 9½" h., Mason's, England, late nineteenth century, $250.00 – 300.00 pair. *Courtesy of JWS.*

Plate 73
Candleholder, Ship's Light, ceramic back plate with brass holder, the brass candleholder allows candle to imply movement of the ship with the waves, interesting piece, $75.00 – 85.00. *Author's Collection.*

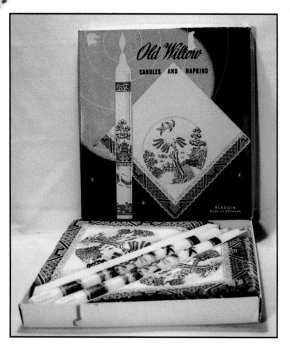

Plate 74

Plate 75

Plate 76

Plate 77

Plate 74
Candle and napkin set, Aladdin, Made in Denmark, $30.00 – 50.00 set. *Courtesy of David R. Harman, Jr.*

Plate 75
Candle and candleholder, unknown maker, candle features Willow pattern, candleholder has, $5.00 – 10.00. *Courtesy of Pam S. Donahue.*

Plate 76
Candle and candleholder, chamber stick type, $5.00 – 10.00 set. *Author's Collection.*

Plate 77
Canister set, graduated sizes, round barrel shape, unmarked, Japanese, $550.00 – 600.00 for complete mint set. *Courtesy of David R. Harman, Jr.*

Plate 78
Canister set, graduated sizes, square shape, unmarked, Japanese, $550.00 – 600.00 for complete mint set. *Courtesy of David R. Harman, Jr.*

Plate 79
Canister set, three stackable pieces with lid, unmarked, Japanese, $125.00. *Courtesy of David R. Harman, Jr.*

Plate 78

Plate 79

Plate 80

Plate 80
Canister set, two shown, four in set, unmarked, Japanese, $250.00 – 350.00. *Courtesy of David R. Harman, Jr.*

Plate 81
Carafe and warmer, 10"h. overall, marked JAPAN, see Mark 86, features removable lid and sits atop a warmer that has an insert for a candle, $200.00 – 250.00. *Author's Collection.*

Plate 82
Carafe and warmer, 12"h. overall, marked, JAPAN, see Mark 86, carafe sits upon a warmer, insert for candle, $175.00 – 200.00. *Author's Collection.*

Plate 81

Plate 82

Plate 83
Canister, 6"h., tin tea canister, W & M, Mansfield, England, $45.00 – 50.00. *Courtesy of Loren Zeller.*

Plate 84
Canister, 6"h., "Instant Coffee" canister, JAPAN, black mark, see Mark 86, $55.00 – 75.00. *Courtesy of David R. Harman, Jr.*

Plate 85
Cat planter, 9¼" l., cat figure, unmarked, Japanese, $275.00 – 300.00+. *Courtesy of Pam S. Donahue.*

Plate 86
Chamber pot, 8¼"d., 5¼"l. unmarked, English, olive green Willow, beautiful, $300.00 – 325.00. *Courtesy of David R. Harman, Jr.*

Plate 83

Plate 85

Plate 84

Plate 86

Plate 87

Plate 88

Plate 89

Plate 90

Plate 91

Plate 87
Chamber pot, Mintons, see Mark 50, English, $275.00 – 300.00. *Author's Collection.*

Plate 88
Chamber pot, 9"d., 5½"h., Doulton & Co., Ltd., Burslem, England, see Mark 22, beautiful, brilliant coloring, $200.00 – 250.00.

Plate 89
Chamber pot, 12"h. to knob, unmarked, English, standard (traditional) Willow pattern, traditional border, immense piece, $425.00 – 525.00. *Courtesy of David R. Harman, Jr.*

Plate 90
Cheese dome, "Stilton," 12"h. to top of handle, 10"d., unmarked, English, grand rare piece, probably had a base for the cheese, $1,500.00+. *Courtesy of Jackie Casey.*

Plate 91
Cheese set, 9" x 5", two Willow inserts and knife, unmarked, Japanese, $55.00 – 85.00.

Plate 92
Cheese dish, covered, G.L. Ashworth & Bros., after 1880, see Mark 7, $200.00 – 225.00. *Courtesy of Pam S. Donahue.*

Plate 92

Plate 93

Plate 94

Plate 93
Cheese dish, covered, Moriyama, Japan, see Mark 95, $175.00 – 200.00. *Courtesy of David R. Harman, Jr.*

Plate 94
Cheese dish, covered, 10"d., 7¼"h., pink/red, made by Regal, England, see Mark 55, $75.00 – 100.00. *Courtesy of David R. Harman, Jr.*

Plate 95
Cheese dish, covered, Gibson & Sons, Ltd., see Mark 26, $175.00 – 200.00. *Author's Collection.*

Plate 96
Child's sugar and creamer, unmarked, Japanese, gold handles, $15.00 – 20.00.

Plate 95

Plate 96

Plate 97

Plate 97
Child's tureen, Japanese, part of set, marked Japan, see Mark 99, $15.00 – 20.00. *Courtesy of David R. Harman, Jr.*

Plate 98
Chocolate pot or demitasse coffeepot, unmarked, Japanese, $50.00 – 75.00. Creamer, 3¼", unmarked, Japanese; sugar, 3¼" h., unmarked, Japanese; $15.00 – 20.00 each. *Courtesy of David R. Harman, Jr.*

Plate 99
Clock, 7¼"d., unmarked, American, hole drilled into plate, inserted clock mechanism, adhered clock numbers, $65.00 – 85.00. *Courtesy of David R. Harman, Jr.*

Plate 100
Coaster set, 4½"d. (coaster), impressed English Ironstone Tableware, Ltd., set of 12 ceramic coasters on a silver rack, $75.00 – 100.00. *Courtesy of David R. Harman, Jr.*

Plate 101
Coaster, 4"d., advertisement for "Yorkshire Relish," English, unmarked, also has the words "Thick or Thin" on the bottom, $45.00 – 55.00. *Courtesy of David R. Harman, Jr.*

Plate 102
Coffeepot, 11½"h., early coffeepot, c. 1790 – 1800, unmarked, $500.00+. *Courtesy of Loren Zeller.*

Plate 98

Plate 100

Plate 99

Plate 101

Plate 102

Plate 103

Plate 104

Plate 105

Plate 106

Plate 107

Plate 108

Plate 106
Compote, 10¼"d., 2¼"h., unmarked, English, footed rim, possibly for cakes, cheeses, or fruits, $275.00 – 300.00. *Courtesy of Pam S. Donahue.*

Plate 107
Compote, 9"d., 6"h., J. Dimmock & Co., Hanley, c. 1862 – 1878, see Mark 21, footed, standard (traditional) Willow pattern, traditional border on underneath of plate and base of pedestal, $150.00 – 175.00. *Author's Collection.*

Plate 108
Compote, 8¾"d., 3½"h., black with gold pattern, Booths Silicon China, England, c. 1906+, $750.00+. *Courtesy of JWS.*

Plate 109

Plate 110

Plate 109
Compote, 7"d., 3½"h., Shenango China, Newcastle, PA, see Mark 125, $60.00 – 75.00. *Courtesy of David R. Harman, Jr.*

Plate 110
Compote, 9½"d., 3"h., Doulton 1882 – 1891, "Persian Spray" with Blue Willow medallions, also known as "Willow & Aster," very rare and beautiful pattern with four different medallions on a 1½" cobalt border and gold decoration, $375.00 – 595.00. *Courtesy of Mikhail and Paul Berkley, Canada.*

Plate 111
Condiment cruet set, approximately 5"h., Prestopan, set of four condiment servers: vinegar (missing lid), salt (missing lid), pepper, and mustard (not shown). Traditional border, English, unmarked, commonly known as "Prestopans" since they were first made in the early to mid-1800s in Prestopan, Scotland. Complete set of four, $1,200.00; individually, $275.00+. *Courtesy of Pam S. Donahue.*

Plate 112
Condiment cruet rack, oil and vinegar, double spout, salt and pepper, funnel, salad fork and spoon, Japanese, wooden rack has holders for each piece, lovely set, $300.00 – 350.00+.

Plate 111

Plate 112

Plate 113

Plate 113
Condiment cruet rack, oil and vinegar, double spout, salt and pepper, funnel, salad fork and spoon, Japanese, paper label, similar to plate, notice the different design on the fork and spoon, $300.00 – 350.00.

Plate 114
Condiment cruet set, round holder, 7½"h., oil, vinegar, salt, pepper, and mustard, with small spoon, Japanese, $300.00 set. *Author's Collection.*

Plate 115
Condiment cruet set, plastic (wooden look) with ceramic oil, vinegar, salad fork and spoon, salt and pepper, and box marked Hostess set by Aladdin, $25.00 – 35.00. *Author's Collection.*

Plate 114

Plate 115

Plate 117

Plate 116

Plate 118

Plate 116
Cookie jar, 9"h., Nelson McCoy Pottery, Roseville, Ohio, see Mark 118, shaped like a pitcher, white pottery with a round decal, traditional variant Willow pattern, $55.00 – 65.00. *Courtesy of David R. Harman, Jr.*

Plate 117
Cookware, 10½"d. handle to handle, unmarked, granite ware, Willow variant, floral, $75.00 – 95.00. *Courtesy of Pam S. Donahue.*

Plate 118
Cookware, 8"l., loaf pan, unmarked, white glass with portion of Willow pattern on front of glass pan, $35.00 – 55.00. *Courtesy of Pam S. Donahue.*

Plate 119
Creamer, cow figure with milkmaid on stool, 7½"l., 6"h., one of a pair of Staffordshire figures, nineteenth century, c. 1860 – 1880, hand-painted details along with Blue Willow transfer, beautiful, $2,500.00+. *Courtesy of Loren Zeller.*

Plate 119

Plate 120
Creamer, cow figure, 7"l., unmarked, English, c. mid-nineteenth century, fitted lid, Blue Willow transfer and hand–painted details, lovely, $1,500.00 – $1,600.00. *Courtesy of Jeanne Berlew.*

Plate 121
Creamer, cow figure, 6½" l., marked Staffordshire ware, Kent, made in England, hand-painted details with Blue Willow transfer, missing fitted lid, see Mark 39, $1,200.00 – 1,400.00 with lid. *Courtesy of David R. Harman, Jr.*

Plate 122
Creamer, 3¼"h., marked in blue, Made In Japan, see Mark 98, $15.00 – 20.00. *Courtesy of David R. Harman, Jr.*

Plate 123
Creamer, 3¼"h., marked Moriyama, Made in Japan, see Mark 95, $50.00 – 55.00. *Courtesy of David R. Harman, Jr.*

Plate 120

Plate 121

Plate 122

Plate 123

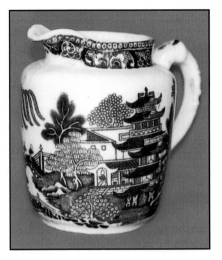

Plate 124

Plate 125

Plate 124
Creamer, 3¾"h., marked Wedgwood & Co., see Mark 70, Two Temples II pattern, $65.00 – 95.00. *Courtesy of David R. Harman, Jr.*

Plate 125
Creamer, 3¾"h., unmarked, English, $35.00 – 50.00. *Courtesy of David R. Harman, Jr.*

Plate 126
Creamer, 3½"h., marked Sadler, see Mark 63, no border, $45.00 – 75.00. *Courtesy of David R. Harman, Jr.*

Plate 127
Creamer, 4"h., marked Tuscan, England, see Mark 68, Mandarin pattern, Dagger border, fluted, rope - like handle, scalloped rim, with gold trim, $65.00 – 75.00. *Courtesy of David R. Harman, Jr.*

Plate 126

Plate 127

Plate 128

Plate 129

Plate 128
Creamer, 3¾"h., unmarked, traditional border inside rim, dark blue coloring against brilliant white, $15.00 – 20.00. *Courtesy of David R. Harman, Jr.*

Plate 129
Creamer, 3¾" h., marked Willow, Grindley, England, hotel ware, traditional border, see Mark 30, $45.00 – 65.00. *Courtesy of David R. Harman, Jr.*

Plate 130
Creamer, 3¾"h., marked Sadler, England, fluted, gold trim, see Mark 63, $45.00 – 55.00. *Courtesy of David R. Harman, Jr.*

Plate 131
Creamer, 3¾"h., Ridgways, England, see Mark 57, bamboo leaf design by handle, $65.00 – 75.00. *Courtesy of David R. Harman, Jr.*

Plate 130

Plate 131

Plate 132

Plate 133

Plate 132
Creamer, 3¾"h., marked Wood & Sons, see Mark 76, $35.00 – 45.00. *Courtesy of David R. Harman, Jr.*

Plate 133
Creamer, 4½"h., marked Booths, see Mark 12, Booths pattern, Bow Knot border, $35.00 – 45.00. *Courtesy of David R. Harman, Jr.*

Plate 134
Creamer, 3½"h., Alfred Meakin, see Mark 46, $55.00 – 75.00. *Courtesy of David R. Harman, Jr.*

Plate 135
Creamer, 3"h., individual, unmarked, American, abbreviated border, $15.00 – 20.00. *Courtesy of David R. Harman, Jr.*

Plate 134

Plate 135

Plate 136

Plate 137

Plate 136
Creamers, individual, no handles, hotel ware, borderless, left to right: 2¼" h., unmarked; 2"h., Shenango, see Mark 125e; 2"h, Shenango; 2"h., Shenango, see Mark 125; 1¾"h., Shenango, see Mark 124. $25.00 – 35.00 each. *Courtesy of David R. Harman, Jr.*

Plate 137
Creamers, individual, handles, borderless, left to right: 3"h., Buffalo China, impressed with Buffalo and words "Buffalo China"; 2¾" h., Shenango, see Mark 125c; 2½"h., Shenango, see Mark 125d; 2"h., Jackson China, see Mark 112; 2"h., Shenango, see Mark 125e; $25.00 – 35.00 each. *Courtesy of David R. Harman, Jr.*

Plate 138

Plate 138
Creamer/open sugar, individual size, 2¼"h. creamer, 3"d. sugar, marked Wood & Sons, see Mark 75; creamer, see Mark 77, $45.00 – 50.00 for set. *Courtesy of David R. Harman, Jr.*

Plate 139
Crisper, 10"h., marked "Blue Magic Krispy Kan, The Luce Corp., South Norwak, Conn.," $45.00 – 55.00. *Courtesy of David R. Harman, Jr.*

Plate 140
Cup/saucer, bouillon/cream soup, 6½" handle to handle, 6¾"d. saucer, marked Old Chinese Willow, made for Henry Morgan & Co., England, see Mark 54, $35.00 – 45.00. *Courtesy of David R. Harman, Jr.*

Plate 139

Plate 140

Plate 141
Cup, child's drinking cup, 3 ⅛" d., 2 ⅛" h., Bourne & Leigh, see Mark 13, $295.00 – 495.00. *Courtesy of Jeanne Berlew.*

Plate 142
Cup/saucer, used for chili, 4"h., 7½" d., unmarked, Japanese, inside features a temple motif, $50.00 – 55.00. *Courtesy of Paul and Bonnie Houck.*

Plate 143
Cup, custard, 3"h, footed, marked Shenango China, New Castle, PA, see Mark 123, $15.00 – 20.00. *Courtesy of David R. Harman, Jr.*

Plate 144
Cups, custard, left: 2½"h., Sterling China Company, Wellsville, Ohio, USA, see Mark 126; right: 2¼"h., Jackson China Company, Falls Creek, Pennsylvania, USA, see Mark 112; both red Willow, standard (traditional) Willow, borders on interiors of cups. $8.00 – 12.00 each. *Courtesy of David R. Harman III.*

Plate 141

Plate 142

Plate 143

Plate 144

Plate 145

Plate 146

Plate 147

Plate 148

Plate 145

Cup, chowder, lid, 3¾" h., 6"d., saucer, Mintons, see Mark 50, $75.00 – 100.00. *Courtesy of David R. Harman, Jr.*

Plate 146

Cup, demitasse, 2½"h., and saucer, Made in Japan, see Mark 90, dark blue coloring, $30.00 – 35.00. *Courtesy of Paul and Bonnie Houck.*

Plate 147

Cup, demitasse, 2¼"h., John Maddock & Sons Ltd., England, see Mark 43, $35.00 – 55.00. *Courtesy of David R. Harman, Jr.*

Plate 148

Cup, juice, 3¾"h., red Mandarin pattern, Copeland Spode, England, c. 1920s, scalloped rim, beautiful, $75.00 – 100.00. *Courtesy of JWS.*

Plate 149

Plate 149
Cups, measuring, 1 cup, ¼ cup, ⅓ cup, ¾ cup (not shown), wooden handles, unmarked, Japanese, lips for easy pouring, $175.00+ for complete set.

Plate 150
Cup, mug, 5 ½" h., unmarked, English, c. 1850s, outside impressed with leaf and block design, $395.00+. *Courtesy of JWS.*

Plate 151
Cup, mug, 4"h., "Imperial Pint," pale blue, Two Temples II pattern, unmarked, English, c. late twentieth century, $395.00+. *Courtesy of JWS.*

Plate 150

Plate 151

Plate 154

Plate 152

Plate 153

Plate 152
Cup, mug, 4½"h., Imperial half-pint, pale blue, unmarked, English, c. 1850 – 1860s, $395.00+. *Courtesy of Loren Zeller.*

Plate 153
Cups, mugs, 3½"h., called "farmer mugs" because of their sturdy construction, unmarked, Japanese, $20.00 – 25.00 each. *Courtesy of Paul and Bonnie Houck.*

Plate 154
Cup, mug, 3½"h., farmer mug, heavy, marked Grant Crest, Japan, see Mark 83, $20.00 – 25.00. *Courtesy of David R. Harman, Jr.*

Plate 155
Cup, mug, 3½"h., unmarked, Japanese, "Mother" printed between two birds on interior, $35.00 – 45.00. *Courtesy of David R. Harman, Jr.*

Plate 156
Cup, mug, 4"h., interesting pattern designed by Philippa Mitchell, see Mark 133, called "Afternoon Tea," features different Booths pattern Willow ware, a teapot, teacup, plate, creamer, sugar, vase, two-tiered server, menu, some lemons, and yellow roses, $10.00. *Author's Collection.*

Plate 157
Cups, mugs, 3½"h, farmer mugs, black mark, JAPAN, $25.00 – 35.00 each. *Courtesy of David R. Harman, Jr.*

Plate 155

Plate 156

Plate 157

Plate 158

Plate 158
Cups, punch, 3¼" h., unmarked, English, Two Temples II pattern, Butterfly border, footed, pedestal, $65.00 – 75.00 each. *Courtesy of David R. Harman, Jr.*

Plate 159
Cup, punch, 3" h., unmarked, footed, pedestal, $60.00 – 65.00. *Courtesy of David R. Harman, Jr.*

Plate 160
Cup, tea, and saucer, gold trim, Thomas C. Wild & Sons, England, see Mark 74, bone china, Mikado, pink Willow, $45.00 – 65.00. *Author's Collection.*

Plate 159

Plate 160

Plate 161

Plate 162

Plate 163

Plate 161
Cup, tea, 2¼"h., and saucer, 5¼"d., three gold feet, two-handled, gold dots and gold trim on interior of cup and on saucer, marked Davenport, Longport, Staffordshire, standard printed mark, c. 1870 – 1887, see Mark 23, Butterfly border on inside rim of cup, interesting piece, $75.00 – 100.00. *Author's Collection.*

Plate 162
Cup, tea, and saucer, pale blue, gold trim, Two Temples II pattern with Butterfly border, unmarked, English, $50.00 – 75.00. *Author's Collection.*

Plate 163
Cup, tea, 4¼"h., and saucer, Royal Winton, by Grimwades, Ltd., Stoke, England, c. 1951+, see Mark 29, Pekin pattern on black background, $100.00 – 125.00.

Plate 164
Cup, tea, and saucer, hand–painted porcelain, gold trim, porcelain, marked "Hand–painted in Occupied Japan," $45.00 – 55.00.

Plate 165
Cup, tea, and saucer, unmarked, Japanese, Two Temples II pattern, $35.00 – 45.00.

Plate 166
Cup, tea, 3½" h., and saucer, 7¾"d., "Take ye a cuppe o'kindness, for auld lang syne," marked Buffalo, see Mark 107, $125.00 mint. *Author's Collection.*

Plate 167
Cup, tea, 2¼"h., 6"d., and saucer, marked Spode, Copeland's, England, gold trim, "We'll Take a Cup O'Kindness Yet for Days O'Auld Lang Syne," $75.00 – 100.00. *Courtesy of David R. Harman, Jr.*

Plate 164

Plate 165

Plate 166

Plate 167

Plate 168
Cup, tea, and saucer, marked "C.B.S. School," Crickman Baptist Church School in Somerset, unmarked, English, c. 1864, $110.00 – 125.00. *Courtesy of JWS.*

Plate 169
Cup, tea, 2½"h., unmarked, Japanese, interior between birds reads " Father" on one cup and "Mother" on the other, $35.00 – 50.00 each. *Courtesy of David R. Harman, Jr.*

Plate 170
Cup, tea, 3¼"h., unmarked, gold trim, spiral design, $35.00 – 45.00. *Courtesy of David R. Harman, Jr.*

Plate 171
Cup, tea, 4"d., 2¼"h., marked Moriyama, Made in Japan, see Mark 95, dark blue color, $50.00 – 55.00. *Courtesy of David R. Harman, Jr.*

Plate 168

Plate 169

Plate 170

Plate 171

Plate 172

Plate 173

Plate 174

Plate 175

Plate 172
Cup, oversized, 5"d., 3¾"h., porcelain, made by Crown Staffordshire Porcelain Co. Ltd., Chinese Willow pattern, marked Chinese Willow, c. 1906+, see Mark 19, $55.00 – 60.00.

Plate 173
Cup, oversized, called a "Texas cup" due to its large size, unmarked, Japanese $35.00 – 45.00, *Courtesy of David R. Harman, Jr.*

Plate 174
Cup, oversized, soup, unmarked, Japanese, $55.00 – 75.00. *Courtesy of David R. Harman, Jr.*

Plate 175
Cup, two–handled child's chocolate cup, 2¼"h, unmarked, English, c. 1840s, $125.00+. *Courtesy of JWS.*

Plate 176

Plate 176

Spirit decanters, very rare and beautiful, three decanters each marked on the front with a letter; B for Brandy, SW for Scotch whiskey, IW for Irish whiskey; impressed registration diamond on the base for 1877 and impressed mark of CF which may indicate Charles Ford – Staffordshire, Pottery. Each has a cork and handle, $2,500.00 – 3,000.00 for set. *Courtesy of Jackie Casey.*

Plate 177

Dessert center piece, 13½"l., 8"w., 5"h, early Mason, c. 1800+, Scroll and Flower border, beautiful multicolored Willow with gold accents, two views shown, $975.00 – 1,200.00. *Courtesy of Loren Zeller.*

Plate 177

Plate 177

Plate 178

Plate 179

Plate 178
Dessert service, John Maddock & Sons, Ltd., England, 1896 – 1921, also marked "Royal Willow," see Mark 44a, $1,200.00+. *Courtesy of Loren Zeller.*

Plate 179
Dishes, 3¼" x 3¾", square stackable dishes, Thomas Cone Ltd., England, see Mark 15, possibly part of a set, $75.00 – 100.00 set. *Courtesy of Brenda Osmer.*

Plate 180
Dish, dresser box or refrigerator box, with lid, 11"l., 6½" h., marked Moriyama, Made in Japan, see Mark 95,

Plate 180

Plate 181

Plate 182

Plate 183

Plate 184

Plate 181
Dish, dresser box or refrigerator box, 8"l., 4½"h., marked Moriyama, Made in Japan, see Mark 95, $150.00 – 175.00. *Author's Collection.*

Plate 182
Dish, dresser box, 4"d, marked Moriyama, Made in Japan, see Mark 95, border is on the lid, lovely piece, $75.00 – 100.00. *Courtesy of David R. Harman, Jr.*

Plate 183
Dish, dresser box, egg shaped, unmarked, Japanese, $125.00. *Courtesy of Pam S. Donahue.*

Plate 184
Dish, dresser box, egg shaped, unmarked, Japanese, gold trim on rim, $125.00. *Courtesy of David R. Harman, Jr.*

Plate 185

Plate 186

Plate 187

Plate 187

Plate 185

Dish, dresser box, 4"d., 1¾"h., gold trim, marked Hillchurch Pottery, Staffordshire, England, see Mark 31, $45.00 – 50.00. *Courtesy of David R. Harman, Jr.*

Plate 186

Dish, leaf dish, 6"l., unmarked, English, leaf shape, also called nut, pickle, or relish dish, $150.00 – 175.00. *Courtesy of David R. Harman, Jr.*

Plate 187

Dish, lid, 4"d., marked Moriyama, Made in Japan, see Mark 95, possibly a small refrigerator box, $90.00 – 100.00. *Author's Collection.*

Plate 188

Plate 189

Plate 190

Plate 191

Plate 192

Plate 188

Dish, 5½"d., Royal Winton by Grimwades, Ltd., Stoke, England, c. 1951+, see Mark 29, possibly a bon bon dish, Pekin pattern, black background, $110.00 – 135.00. *Courtesy of Pam S. Donahue.*

Plate 189

Dish, 3½" x 4½", pin dish, Royal Winton by Grimwades, Ltd., Stoke, England, c. 1951+, see Mark 29, Pekin pattern, black background, $110.00 – 135.00. *Courtesy of Pam S. Donahue.*

Plate 190

Dish, strawberry, 12½"x 8¼", strawberry handles, Mason's, beautiful and rare piece, $850.00+. *Courtesy of JWS.*

Plate 191

Drainer, 4½" square, butter, unmarked, English, $75.00 – 100.00. *Courtesy of David R. Harman, Jr.*

Plate 192

Drainer, 3½", butter, round, unmarked, English, $75.00 – 100.00. *Courtesy of David R. Harman, Jr.*

Plate 193

Drainer, 3½", butter, round, unmarked, English, $75.00 – 100.00. *Courtesy of David R. Harman, Jr.,*

Plate 193

Plate 194

Plate 194

Drainer, 13½"d., meat drainer, Temple-Landscape I pattern, as described in Robert Copeland's *Spode's Willow Pattern and Other Designs After the Chinese*, page 97. Lattice and dagger border (similar to Mandarin border) with unusual inner border, mid-eighteenth century, "Nanking Cargo" (Nanking is a port in China, see glossary), packed in tea, purchased at auction at Christi's, $250.00+. *Courtesy of Eileen Callow.*

Plate 195

Drainer, 18"d., meat, four areas of small landscapes, background of floral motifs, design is similar to the Net pattern as described in Robert Copeland's *Spode's Willow Pattern and Other Designs After the Chinese*, pages 90 – 91, $350.00+. *Courtesy of Eileen Callow.*

Plate 195

Plate 196

Plate 197

Plate 196
Dresser set, green, Willow variant on glass, unmarked, part of a set, also seen with candlesticks, lovely set, $850.00 – 1,200.00+. *Courtesy of Pam S. Donahue.*

Plate 197
Egg cups, 3½"h., marked Japan in black, front and back shown, see Mark 98, $30.00 – 35.00 each. *Courtesy of Paul and Bonnie Houck.*

Plate 198

Plate 199

Plate 200

Plate 201

Plate 202

Plate 203

Plate 198
Cups, 4"h., unmarked, English, red Willow, standard (traditional) Willow pattern and border, photo shows back and front of pattern, $35.00 – 45.00 each. *Courtesy of David R. Harman III.*

Plate 199
Egg cup, 3½"h., unmarked, hand-painted, variant pattern, $35.00 – 40.00. *Courtesy of Pam S. Donahue.*

Plate 200
Egg cup, 3¾"h., metal top, for "coddled eggs," Worcester pattern, Scroll and Flower border, English, $125.00 – 130.00. *Courtesy of Pam S. Donahue.*

Plate 201
Egg cup, 3¾"h., metal top, for "coddled eggs," Worcester pattern, Scroll and Flower border, English, $125.00 – 130.00. *Courtesy of Pam S. Donahue.*

Plate 202
Egg cup stand, 5½"h., unmarked, early English, c. 1820 – 1840, Two Temples II pattern, six original cups, fantastic "twisted" handle, $1,500.00 – 2,000.00. *Courtesy of Loren Zeller.*

Plate 203
Egg cup stand, unmarked, English, resembles a basket, base has the appearance of basket weave, gold trim, beautiful, $900.00 – 1,200.00. *Courtesy of David R. Harman, Jr.*

Plate 203

Plate 204

Plate 204
Flatware, 6-pc. ice drink spoons, stainless steel and melamine handles, $25.00 – 35.00. *Courtesy of David R. Harman, Jr.*

Plate 205
Flour sifter, metal, 6"h., $55.00 – 75.00. *Courtesy of Pam S. Donahue.*

Plate 206
Garden seat, 18"h., 44½"d., lovely large item to set in the garden, unmarked, $125.00.

Plate 205

Plate 206

Plate 207

Plate 208

Plate 209

Plate 207
Ginger jar, 5¼"h., unmarked, Japanese, brown Willow, $75.00 – 85.00. *Courtesy of Pam S. Donahue.*

Plate 208
Ginger jar, 5"h., Bristol, Made in England, R. Twining & Co., Ltd. of London, red Willow, missing lid, $65.00 – 75.00. *Courtesy of William and Vitalia Hodgetts.*

Plate 209
Ginger jar, 5¼"h., Mason's, lovely variant item, lid has Scroll and Flower border, $45.00 – 55.00. *Courtesy of David R. Harman, Jr.*

Plate 210

Plate 211

Plate 212

Plate 210

Glass tumbler, full, Blue Plate Foods, founded in 1925, now known as Reily Foods Company, traditional pattern plate logo on paper label on glass, advertising peanut butter, "Creamy Blend," also features a "Buzzy Bunny" character on tumbler, $35.00 – 45.00. *Courtesy of Pam S. Donahue.*

Plate 211

Glass sauce containers, Blue Plate Foods, feature the traditional pattern plate logo on paper labels on glass containers. Left: Blue Plate Worcestershire Sauce, USA, original contents, 7 ¼"h.; right: Blue Plate Steak Sauce, USA, 7 ¾"h. $ND. *Courtesy of JWS.*

Plate 212

Glass food containers, two cooking sauce jars with the Blue Willow design on the paper label. Left: Thai Curry; right: Peking Yellow Bean. Original price tags, $7.99. *Courtesy of Pam S. Donahue.*

Plate 213

Plate 214

Plate 213
Glass ginger jar and water glasses. Covered jar, 5¼"h., Hawke's. Water glasses, 5¾"h., Hawke's. Willow pattern cut in glass, beautiful pieces. Covered jar, $595.00+; water glasses, $125.00+ each. *Courtesy of Pam S. Donahue.*

Plate 214
Glass decanter, 9¾"h., and glasses, left to right: 4¼" stem, 5" water, 7¼" wine, stem; Willow patterns cut in glass. Stevens and Williams, c. 1920 – 1940s. Decanter, $500.00+, glasses $95.00 – 110.00 each. *Courtesy of Pam S. Donahue.*

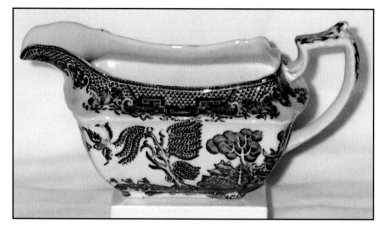

Plate 215

Plate 216

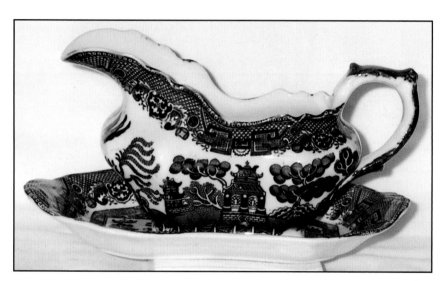

Plate 217

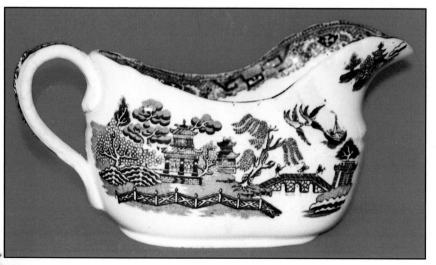

Plate 218

Plate 215
Gravy boat, 6" spout to handle, 4"h., unmarked, English, attributed to Spode, $125.00+. *Courtesy of Jeanne Berlew.*

Plate 216
Gravy boat, 7¾" spout to handle, Globe Pottery Co., England, c. pre-1917, see Mark 27, $75.00 – 85.00. *Courtesy of Jeanne Berlew.*

Plate 217
Gravy boat, 8" spout to handle, liner 8½" x 4½", Allerton, England, c. 1929 – 1942, see Mark 4, scalloped rim and base, lovely, $95.00 – 100.00. *Courtesy of Jeanne Berlew.*

Plate 218
Gravy boat, 8" spout to handle, E.B. & J.E.L., Bourne & Leigh, Burslem, England, c. 1892 – 1939, see Mark 13, $65.00 – 85.00. *Courtesy of David R. Harman, Jr.*

Plate 219

Plate 220

Plate 219
Gravy boat, 7½" spout to handle, Maestricht, Holland, see Mark 136, red Willow $50.00 – 65.00. *Courtesy of Pam S. Donahue.*

Plate 220
Gravy boat, 6½" spout to spout, 8" handle to handle, liner, unmarked, American, the Royal China Company, Sebring, Ohio, $20.00 – 25.00 set. *Courtesy of Paul and Bonnie Houck.*

Plate 221
Gravy boat, 4"h. to spout, 9"d., unmarked, liner for the Homer Laughlin China Company, marked H.L. B44 N6, see Mark 115, $25.00 – 35.00. *Courtesy of Paul and Bonnie Houck.*

Plate 221

Plate 222

Plate 223

Plate 224

Plate 222
Gravy dish, 6" spout to handle, traditional pattern, no border, Shenango China Co., $15.00 – 25.00. *Courtesy of David R. Harman, Jr.*

Plate 223
Gravy boat, 7¼" spout to spout, 8½"d., Alfred Meakin, England, see Mark 46, attached liner, interesting mark, old Willow, design of bridge with three people crossing it, gravy boat and liner are one piece, molded together, $50.00 – 75.00. *Courtesy of David R. Harman, Jr.*

Plate 224
Gravy dish, 6"d. spout to spout, "Gravy" and "Lean" printed on interior with partial design handle in back for easy pouring, great item, $75.00 – 100.00. *Author's Collection.*

Plate 225

Plate 225
Hot pots, left to right: 6"h., 8½"h., rosebud finial, electric, unmarked, Japanese, $65.00 – 85.00 each.

Plate 226
Jam jar, 3"h., Japanese, see Mark 86, lid, $25.00 – 30.00. *Courtesy of David R. Harman, Jr.*

Plate 227
Jam jar, bamboo handle, unmarked, Japanese, porcelain, 1990s, $15.00 – 20.00.

Plate 227

Plate 226

Plate 228
Jam jar, 4"h., unmarked, Japanese, two handles, lid, $35.00 – 45.00. *Courtesy of David R. Harman, Jr.*

Plate 229
Jam jar, 3"h., marked Willow, "knot" England, unknown English company, silverplated lid with knob, $45.00 – 55.00. *Courtesy of David R. Harman, Jr.*

Plate 230
Jam jars, 3½"h., hand-painted variant pattern, marked Lancaster & Sandland Ltd., Hanley, England, 1949+, see Mark 41, $60.00 – 75.00 set. *Courtesy of Pam S. Donahue.*

Plate 231
Jardiniere, 6"h., with an opening of 5¾", marked Mintons, Mark 49, Flow Blue, gorgeous piece, $895.00 – 1,200.00+. *Courtesy of Jackie Casey.*

Plate 228

Plate 229

Plate 230

Plate 231

Plate 232

Plate 232
Jardiniere, 8"d., Lancaster & Sandland Ltd., Hanley, England, c. 1949+, see Mark 41, hand-painted variant pattern, $125.00 – 145.00. *Courtesy of Pam S. Donahue.*

Plate 233
Jewelry, brass pin, in plastic case, $ND. *Courtesy of Pam S. Donahue.*

Plate 234
Jewelry, pins, ceramic and metal, each has different Willow motif, brooch type pins, $ND. *Courtesy of Pam S. Donahue.*

Plate 233

Plate 234

Plate 235

Plate 236

Plate 237

Plate 235
Jewelry, pins, ceramic and metal, all show portions of the Willow pattern, the three multicolored pins are from a variant Willow pattern piece, $ND. *Courtesy of Pam S. Donahue.*

Plate 236
Jewelry, pins, one reads "Blue Willow collector," one is a mini version of the traditional Willow plate, one is a teapot shape, $ND. *Courtesy of Pam S. Donahue.*

Plate 237
Jewelry box, variant Willow pattern on lid, filled with Willow jewelry, open and closed views, $ND. *Courtesy of Pam S. Donahue.*

Plate 237

Plate 238

Plate 239

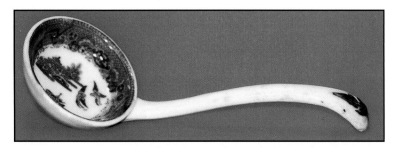

Plate 240

Plate 241

Plate 238
Juice set, 8½"h. pitcher, 3½"h. tumblers, unmarked, Japanese, $175.00 – 200.00 set, $15.00 – 20.00 tumblers, $75.00 – 100.00 pitcher. *Courtesy of Paul and Bonnie Houck.*

Plate 239
Juicer or reamer, 1990s, $15.00 – 25.00. *Courtesy of Gary and Sandy Osenbaugh.*

Plate 240
Ladle, 8½"l., 2¾"d., unmarked, English, traditional border, two birds, boat with one figure, small landscape scene, lovely item, handle has a blue floral design at bend, $275.00 – 300.00. *Courtesy of David R. Harman, Jr.*

Plate 241
Ladle, 8½"l., 2¾"d., unmarked, English, traditional border only on interior rim of ladle, diamond design on molded handle, $275.00 – 300.00. *Courtesy of David R. Harman, Jr.*

Plate 242

Plate 243

Plate 244

Plate 242
Lavabo set, two pieces, 9½"l., top, 7¼"w., 3½" deep, bottom, unmarked, Japanese, $150.00 – 175.00. *Courtesy of Pam S. Donahue.*

Plate 243
Lamp, kerosene, 11"h., black/gold JAPAN paper label, nice shape and gold trim, $120.00 – 125.00. *Courtesy of David R. Harman, Jr.*

Plate 244
Lamp, kerosene, 10"h., unmarked, Japanese, gold trim, round base, $95.00 – 110.00. *Courtesy of David R. Harman, Jr.*

Plate 245
Lamp shade, unmarked, Japanese, fits onto a kerosene lamp metal shade holder, $15.00 – 25.00. *Courtesy of David R. Harman, Jr.*

Plate 245

Plate 246

Plate 247

Plate 248

Plate 249

Plate 246
Lamp, electric, appears to be made from a ginger jar, Two Temples II variant pattern, shade material has repeating Willow pattern design, wooden base, four metal feet, $150.00 – 175.00. *Courtesy of David R. Harman, Jr.*

Plate 247
Lamp, electric, 29" h. overall, Pekin pattern on a red background, exquisite, Royal Winton, by Grimwades Ltd., Stoke, England, c. 1951+, see Mark 29, $495.00+. *Courtesy of Pam S. Donahue.*

Plate 248
Lamp, electric, 22¾" h., overall, Pekin pattern on light blue stippled background, brilliant coloring, Royal Winton, by Grimwades Ltd., Stoke, England, c. 1951+, see Mark 29, $495.00+. *Courtesy of Pam S. Donahue.*

Plate 249
Lamps, electric, 26"h. overall, Pekin pattern on dark blue background, beautiful deep colorings, Royal Winton, by Grimwades Ltd., Stoke, England, c. 1951+, see Mark 29, $990.00+ for pair. *Courtesy of Pam S. Donahue.*

Plate 250

Plate 251

Plate 252

Plate 250
Lamp, electric, 9"h., 6"w., unmarked, lovely fringed shade, $150.00+. *Courtesy of William and Vitalia Hodgetts.*

Plate 251
Lamp, electric, 21¼" to top of finial, 10" to top of porcelain, marked "Made in England," c. 1920 – 1930s, metal footed base and finial, lovely porcelain décor, $600.00+. *Courtesy of Jeanne Berlew.*

Plate 252
Lighter, demitasse teacup shape, removable metal lighter, $75.00 – 100.00. *Courtesy of Pam S. Donahue.*

Plate 253

Plate 253
Linens, comforter, orange-brown color, Willow pattern repeated throughout material, $ND. *Courtesy of Pam S. Donahue.*

Plate 254
Linens, canvas carrying cases, assorted examples of Willow pattern, $ND. *Courtesy of Pam S. Donahue.*

Plate 255
Linens, oven mitts, feature repeating Willow pattern, $10.00 – 15.00 pair. *Courtesy of Pam S. Donahue.*

Plate 256
Linens, placemats featuring Willow pattern, fringes, $ND. *Courtesy of Pam S. Donahue.*

Plate 257
Linens, tablecloths, Simtex Mills, New York, NY, features Willow pattern on both, one has different shades of green, the other has different shades of red on white, $50.00 – 100.00 each. *Courtesy of Pam S. Donahue.*

Plate 254

Plate 255

Plate 256

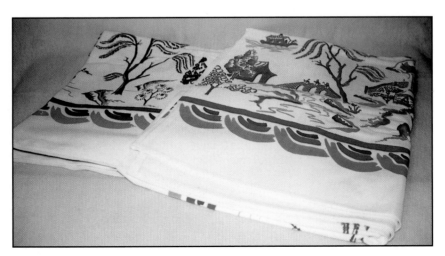

Plate 257

Plate 258

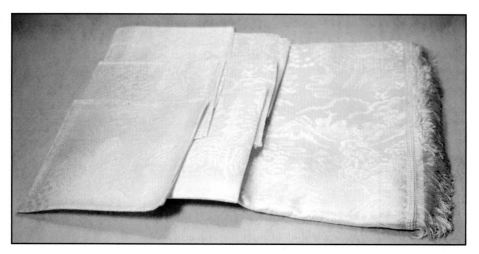

Plate 259

Plate 258
Linens, tablecloth and napkins, Simtex Mills, New York, NY, different shades of blue on white, $50.00 – 100.00 tablecloth, $25.00 – 35.00 set of four napkins. *Courtesy of Pam S. Donahue.*

Plate 259
Linens, tablecloth and napkins, variant Willow pattern on ivory cloth with fringes on the tablecloth, beautiful, $100.00 – 125.00+. *Courtesy of Pam S. Donahue.*

Plate 260
Linens, tea towel, features landscape and temple, $ND. *Courtesy of Pam S. Donahue.*

Plate 261
Linens, tea towel, features colorful scheme of kitchen table setting, window view, cat laying on a stool, and a variant Blue Willow teapot, creamer, sugar, cup and saucer settings, and yummy desserts on the table, $ND. *Courtesy of Pam S. Donahue.*

Plate 260

Plate 261

Plate 263

Plate 262

Plate 262
Miniature tea set, 3½"d., tray, two cups and saucers, creamer, teapot, sugar, two lids, trimmed in gold, $12.00 – 25.00. *Courtesy of Paul and Bonnie Houck.*

Plate 263
Miscellaneous, homemade white slip-on shoes, motifs of the Willow pattern glued onto the shoes with two blue bows, made by Pam Donahue's mother, $ND. *Courtesy of Pam S. Donahue.*

Plate 264
Miscellaneous, photo album, homemade, Blue Willow pattern, material with lace and ribbons, $ND. *Courtesy of Pam S. Donahue.*

Plate 265
Miscellaneous, hat box, homemade, Blue Willow pattern in black, $ND. *Courtesy of Pam S. Donahue.*

Plate 265

Plate 264

Plate 266
Miscellaneous, tea box, $ND. *Courtesy of Pam S. Donahue.*

Plate 267
Miscellaneous, cat with head in teapot, Blue Willow variant pattern, Siamese cat, $12.00 – 15.00. *Courtesy of Pam S. Donahue.*

Plate 268
Miscellaneous, "The Cat's Meow" sill sitter, purchased in Perkins Cove, Maine. Sign advertises "Blue Willow, Gifts and Luncheon Tea Room – Oceanfront Dining," back reads "Created Exclusively for Coves End Oqunquit, Maine," signed by Faline '96. Purchased in 2000 for $14.99. *Author's Collection.*

Plate 266

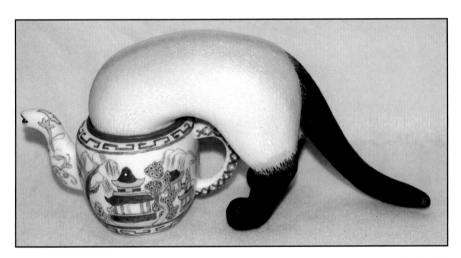

Plate 267

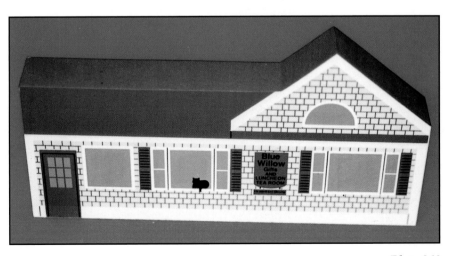

Plate 268

Plate 269

Plate 269
Miscellaneous, matches, business advertisements for a catering company with the name "Blue Willow," $ND. *Courtesy of Pam S. Donahue.*

Plate 270
Muffineers, 5½"h., Moriyama, Japan, see Mark 95, octagonal body shape (top of shaker design is a characteristic commonly seen on knobs of Moriyama, Japan pieces; compare with pancake keeper knob, Plate 281) $175.00 – 200.00 set.

Plate 271
Mustard, covered, 3½"h., marked Buffalo Pottery 1916, see Mark 106, $150.00 – 175.00. *Courtesy of David R. Harman, Jr.*

Plate 272
Mustard, covered, 4½"h., 4½"l., spoon, marked Japan, see Mark 86, spoon has geometric border on handle, $75.00 – 80.00. *Author's Collection.*

Plate 270

Plate 272

Plate 271

106

Plate 273

Plate 274

Plate 273
Mustard, covered, 3"h. to knob, marked The Bailey–Walker Co., c. 1920s – 1940, see Mark 127, lid is slotted for spoon, $55.00 – 65.00. *Author's Collection.*

Plate 274
Napkin holder, 4½"d., 4½"h., unmarked, Japanese, beautiful, $125.00 – 145.00. *Courtesy of David R. Harman, Jr.*

Plate 275
Oil & vinegar set, 7"h., stoppers have portion of Willow pattern on both, marked with a triangle, $35.00. *Courtesy of Paul and Bonnie Houck.*

Plate 275

Plate 276

Plate 277

Plate 278

Plate 276
Oil & vinegar set, 6½"h. overall, paper label, black/gold, Creative Imports, Inc., JAPAN, lids are stoppers with cork, the partial border on the stoppers have fish roe lattice with four circular designs, evenly spaced, the knob has just the lattice design, $55.00 – 65.00 set. *Author's Collection.*

Plate 277
Oil & vinegar set, 5¼"h. overall, marked in black, JAPAN, "OIL" printed on one and "VINEGAR" on the other, $55.00 – 65.00 set. *Courtesy of David R. Harman, Jr.*

Plate 278
Ornaments, left to right: round shape with Willow pattern, holly leaf/berry designs on both sides, and on the back just the two birds; bell shaped with Willow pattern motif, holly leaf/berry designs on top of bell; round shape with circular Willow pattern on both sides, with lovely pink roses/greens on either side centered, 1991 on the bottom in gold, $15.00 each. *Author's Collection.*

Plate 279

Plate 280

Plate 281

Plate 279
Ornament, snowman, Cardew Design, England, see Mark 130, $10.00 new. *Author's Collection.*

Plate 280
Ornament, teapot, Cardew Design, England, see Mark 130, $10.00 new. *Author's Collection.*

Plate 281
Pancake keeper, 10¾" handle to handle, 3¾"h., Moriyama, Japan, see Mark 95, small hole for ventilation on cover, beautiful Willow pattern on cover, two-handled plate also features the Willow pattern in the center, sometimes called a dome cake plate; due to the height and the vent hole it seems more reasonable to call it a pancake keeper. $300.00 – 325.00. *Courtesy of Pam S. Donahue.*

Plate 282

Plate 282
Paper, placemats, 9¾" x 13¼", unmarked, unopened, $10.00 – 15.00. *Courtesy of Pam S. Donahue.*

Plate 283
Paper, stationery set, includes stationery with a scene of the three figures crossing the bridge, the Willow tree, and a part of the temple, matching envelopes, all come in a lovely cardboard folder with the Willow pattern on the front, original price of $11.99 in 1998. *Courtesy of David R. Harman, Jr.*

Plate 284
Pepperette, 5"h., 2½"d., unmarked, English, lovely piece, $150.00 – 175.00. *Courtesy of Glenn and Rosemary Gibbs.*

Plate 285
Perfume bottle, 1¾"d., ½"w., English, porcelain, registered design number 29260, hallmarked silver top, $300.00 – 475.00. *Courtesy of Glenn and Rosemary Gibbs.*

Plate 283

Plate 284

Plate 285

Plate 286

Plate 287

Plate 287

Plate 286
Pillows, 9¼" x 9¼", feature gooseneck spout coffeepot/teapot, with a variant Blue Willow pattern, needlepoint, in shades of blue, white, and gold highlights, velveteen backs with zipper closings, lovely accent pillows for the Willow collector, $55.00 each. *Courtesy of Pam S. Donahue.*

Plate 287
Pitcher, covered, 6¼"d. spout to handle, 5"h., marked Buffalo, see Mark 103, c. 1910, $275.00 – 350.00. *Courtesy of Jeanne Berlew.*

Plate 288

Plate 289

Plate 288

Pitchers, covered, left to right: 6"h. and 5"h., marked Buffalo 1911 and 1910, see Marks 105 and 103, sometimes called syrup jugs although listed as jugs in a 1905 booklet directly from Buffalo Pottery. Lid was removed to display pattern; note pagoda on tip of lid. The company made these in four sizes: 1 pint, 1 pint, 7 ounces, 2 pints, 4 ounces, and 3 pints, 5½ ounces. $275.00 – 350.00 each. *Courtesy of David R. Harman, Jr.*

Plate 289

Pitchers, graduated sizes, 8¼"h., 5½"h., and 3⅞"h., marked Willow, England; see Mark 57, Ridgways, England, Bow/Quiver mark, c. 1912 – 1927, all pieces have bamboo embossed handles. $500.00 – 525.00 set. *Courtesy of Jeanne Berlew.*

Plate 290

Plate 290
Pitcher, closer view of largest pitcher in Plate 289, 8¼"h., note the detail of the bamboo embossed handles. $175.00 – 185.00. *Courtesy of Jeanne Berlew.*

Plate 291
Pitcher, 7¼"h., marked Allerton, England, see Mark 5, scalloped edge and base, elegant piece, $325.00 – 400.00. *Courtesy of Jeanne Berlew.*

Plate 292
Pitcher, 6"h., Booths Silicon China, "Davenport Willow," England, c. 1906+, beautiful example, $425.00 – 525.00. *Courtesy of JWS.*

Plate 291

Plate 292

Plate 293

Plate 294

Plate 295

Plate 296

Plate 293
Pitcher, 6¾" h., unmarked, six–sided shapes, scalloped edge, $150.00. *Courtesy of David R. Harman, Jr.*

Plate 294
Pitcher, 6¾" h., marked Wedgwood & Co., England, see Mark 70, $125.00 – 175.00. *Courtesy of David R. Harman, Jr.*

Plate 295
Pitcher, 6"h., unmarked, English, brown Willow, $95.00 – 125.00. *Courtesy of David R. Harman, Jr.*

Plate 296
Pitcher, 5"h., unmarked, Japanese, $95.00 – 125.00.

Plate 297
Pitcher, 6¼"h., marked in blue, JAPAN, see Mark 99, $75.00 – 95.00. *Courtesy of David R. Harman, Jr.*

Plate 298
Pitcher, 6"h., marked England, Johnson, Willow, see Mark 36, $65.00 – 85.00. *Courtesy of David R. Harman, Jr.*

Plate 297

Plate 298

Plate 299

Plate 300

Plate 301

Plate 299
Pitcher, 8"h., unmarked, Butterfly border, Two Temples II pattern, $250.00 – 300.00. *Courtesy of David R. Harman, Jr.*

Plate 300
Pitcher, 9"h., W.S. George Pottery Company, USA, see Mark 111, c. late 1930s, "Derwood" shape, traditional Willow pattern decal, $75.00 – 100.00. *Courtesy of David R. Harman, Jr.*

Plate 301
Pitchers, left to right: 5½"h., 7"h., James Sadler & Sons, made in England, see Mark 64, gold trim on rims and handles, $125.00 – 150.00 set. *Courtesy of David R. Harman, Jr.*

Plate 302
Pitcher, 5¼"h., marked New Hall, see Mark 52, multicolored decal, front and back views, $75.00 – 100.00. *Courtesy of David R. Harman, Jr.*

Plate 303
Pitchers, left to right: 6"h., unmarked, 4 ¾" h., marked in black, JAPAN, front and back views shown, $55.00 – 75.00 each. *Courtesy of David R. Harman, Jr.*

Plate 302

Plate 302

Plate 303

Plate 304

Plate 305

Plate 306

Plate 307

Plate 308

Plate 309

Plate 304
Pitcher, 6½"h., William Alsager Adderley, England, see Mark 1, $175.00 – 200.00 mint. *Courtesy of Pam S. Donahue.*

Plate 305
Pitcher, 5¼"h., Charles Allerton & Sons, see Mark 5, $100.00 – 125.00. *Courtesy of David R. Harman, Jr.*

Plate 306
Pitcher, 5¼"h., Charles Allerton & Sons, see Mark 5, beautiful pattern, birds placed evenly centered under the spout, $125.00 – 135.00. *Courtesy of David R. Harman, Jr.*

Plate 307
Pitcher, 7"h., Frank Beardmore & Co., Fenton, England, c. 1903 – 1914, see Mark 9, Basaltine Willow, bold multicolored standard (traditional) Willow, on bright blue background, handle, upper edge inside and outside are black, $450.00 – 500.00. *Courtesy of Loren Zeller.*

Plate 308
Pitcher, ice–lip, Hazel Atlas Glass Company, blue and white traditional Willow pattern on clear glass, $55.00 – 65.00. *Courtesy of Pam S. Donahue.*

Plate 309
Pitcher, ice–lip, unknown maker, Blue Willow pattern on frosted glass, $45.00 – 55.00. *Courtesy of Pam S. Donahue.*

Plate 310

Plate 311

Plate 312

Plate 312

Plate 310
Pitcher, 8½"h., unmarked, English, light olive green, beautiful old piece, $450.00 – 500.00. *Courtesy of Jeanne Berlew.*

Plate 311
Pitcher, unmarked, granite ware pitcher, Willow decal, cobalt rim, $25.00 – 35.00. *Courtesy of Pam S. Donahue.*

Plate 312
Place card, 2¾"d., unmarked, English, traditional pattern with a white banner for writing one's guests' names, (this one is missing a portion of the ceramic back), $75.00 – 125.00. *Author's Collection.*

Plate 313
Place setting, Cambridge Glass Company, Cambridge, Ohio. Blue–filled etching on the reverse side causes the traditional Willow pattern and border to appear reversed. This setting has a cake dish, cake plates, footed teacups, saucers, an open sugar bowl, and creamer (missing). A beautiful set, $1,200.00 – 1,500.00. *Courtesy of David R. Harman, Jr.*

Plate 314
Place setting, Royal China Company, Sebring, Ohio, see Mark 120, traditional Willow pattern in brown, set shows 10½" lug plate, sauce bowl, 9" vegetable bowl, and 6" luncheon plate. Lug plate, $20.00 – 25.00; sauce bowl, $6.00 – 8.00; vegetable, $10.00 – 12.00; luncheon plate, $8.00 – 10.00. *Courtesy of Pam S. Donahue.*

Plate 313

Plate 314

Plate 315

Plate 316

Plate 317

Plate 318

Plate 315

Place setting, Royal China Company, Sebring, Ohio, traditional Willow pattern in green on back. Dinner plate, $8.00 – 12.00; grill plate, $15.00 – 18.00; bread plate, $10.00 – 12.00; soup bowl, $12.00 – 15.00; sauce/berry bowl, $6.00 – 8.00; cup/saucer, $8.00 – 10.00; coffee mug, $10.00 – 12.00; salt/pepper, $15.00 – 20.00. *Courtesy of Pam S. Donahue.*

Plate 316

Place setting, Royal China Company, Sebring, Ohio, see Mark 120, traditional Willow pattern in blue on back. Soup, 8¼", $12.00 – 15.00; dinner plate, 10", $8.00 – 12.00; berry bowl, 5½", $7.00 – 8.00; cup, 2½"h., $8.00 – 10.00; saucer, 6", $8.00 – 10.00. *Courtesy of Paul and Bonnie Houck.*

Plate 317

Place setting, cup/saucer, Gold Castle, Made in Japan, see Mark 82, small plate, green, variant pattern, variant Butterfly border, $35.00 – 45.00 set.

Plate 318

Place setting, 6" x 6¼", Royal Winton by Grimwades, Ltd., England, c. 1951, see Mark 29, Pekin pattern, black background, Ascot shape, $115.00 per plate. *Courtesy of Glenn and Rosemary Gibbs.*

Plate 319

Plate 320

Plate 321

Plate 322

Plate 319
Place setting, in box, 16–piece starter set, Made in Japan, black mark, produced by Morisho Seitosho, Yokkaichi, Japan, $175.00 complete set, mint in box.

Plate 320
Plate, advertising, unmarked, multicolored decal, traditional Willow pattern, floral decoration in gold on an interesting shaped border, "W.C. Strause SELLS MEAT THAT GRANDMA CAN EAT," $55.00 – 65.00 (note wear on decal, by birds; price is for mint condition). *Courtesy of David R. Harman, Jr.*

Plate 321
Plate, advertising, 11"d., Sterling China Company, see Mark 126, "Busch's," $85.00 – 100.00. *Author's Collection.*

Plate 322
Plate, advertising, 7½"d., Wedgwood & Co., England. On top of plate, "Ye Olde Cheshire Cheese," on top of the cheese, "145 Fleet Street," and underneath "Wine Office Court," advertisement for a London pub and restaurant, James Green & Nephew (printed part of plate) (see postcards for history) $110.00 – 175.00 (value higher for postcards). *Courtesy of Glenn and Rosemary Gibbs.*

Plate 323
Plate, postcards, first one is numbered 5704, printed and published by Gale & Polden Ltd., 2 Amen Corner EC4. The description is "Ye Olde Cheshire Cheese – The Chop Room," which has brass plates on the walls, showing favorite seats of Dr. Johnson, Charles Dickens, etc. The second reads "Ye Olde Cheshire Cheese – The Crypt being part of the Wine Vaults." Ye Olde Cheshire Cheese pub existed during the mid-seventeenth century and Dr. Samuel Johnson, compiler of the first English dictionary, was a regular customer. The pub also became popular with Charles Dickens, James Thackery, and Mark Twain. $ND. *Courtesy of Glenn and Rosemary Gibbs.*

Plate 324
Plate, advertising, 7"d., unmarked, "My Goodness, My Guinness!"; features two figures on bridge, one on left is carrying a beverage, the other is chasing the first with a sword of some sort; interesting how the Willow tree was "trimmed" to allow room for the figure. $85.00 – 110.00. *Author's Collection.*

Plate 323

Plate 324

Plate 325

Plate 326

Plate 327

Plate 325
Plate, advertising, 10"d., unmarked, "B Hall, Woodstock St & Bond St," c. 1880, $185.00 – 375.00. *Courtesy of Loren Zeller.*

Plate 326
Plate, advertising, 9¾"d., unmarked, English, "London Tavern," c. 1820 – 1840, $185.00 – 375.00. *Courtesy of Loren Zeller.*

Plate 327
Plate, advertising, 10"d., unmarked, English, "WR Ships Tavern Water Lane," c. 1880, $185.00 – 375.00. *Courtesy of Loren Zeller.*

Plate 328

Plate 329

Plate 328
Plate, charger, 12½"d., Royal Winton, by Grimwades Ltd., Stoke, England, c. 1951+, see Mark 29, Pekin pattern, black background, stunning 2½" embossed white borders, a truly unusual and beautiful piece, $275.00 – 325.00. *Courtesy of Agnes and David R. Harman, Jr.*

Plate 329
Plate, 12½"d., charger, Ridgways, England, c. 1900, traditional Willow pattern, yellow transfer print with overpainting, beautiful cobalt blue molded border, Gaudy Willow, $350.00 – 475.00+. *Courtesy of Loren Zeller.*

Plate 330
Plate, chop, 12"d., The Royal China Company, Sebring, Ohio, unmarked, $15.00 – 25.00. *Courtesy of Paul and Bonnie Houck.*

Plate 331
Plate, lug, 10½"d, The Royal China Company, Sebring, Ohio, see Mark 121, two handles, $15.00 – 20.00. *Courtesy of Paul and Bonnie Houck.*

Plate 332
Plates, collector's, 6"d., feature Buster Brown and his dog Tige. In the one on the left, Buster Brown is pouring from a Willow teapot into a Willow teacup held by Tige. The plate on the right features Tige balancing a Willow teapot on his nose and Buster Brown pointing at the dog. $35.00 – 55.00 each.

Plate 331

Plate 330

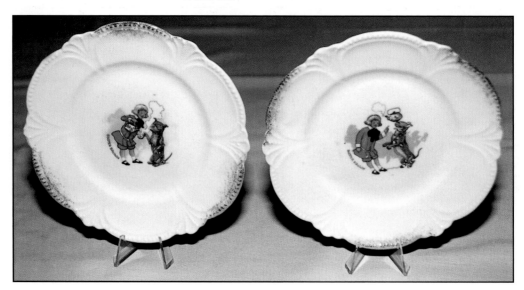

Plate 332

Plate 333

Plate 334

Plate 334

Plate 333
Plate, collector's, 10½"d, Royal Doulton Story plate, one in a series, portrays one part of the Willow legend, issued by Royal Doulton, c. 1920 – 1945, floral border, $125.00 – 150.00. *Courtesy of Loren Zeller.*

Plate 334
Plate, collector's, 6"d., Josiah Wedgwood mark, words read "Children's Story 1971" on top, then, "'The Sandman' by Hans Christian Andersen," scene features the Sandman sitting on the child's bed. Another version of the plate has "Child's Day 1971" at the top. Note the umbrella portrays the Willow pattern, $75.00 – 110.00. *Courtesy of Paul and Bonnie Houck.*

Plate 335

Plate 336

Plate 337

Plate 338

Plate 339

Plate 340

Plate 335
Plate, Depression glass, 11½"d., unmarked, decorative salad–type plate, gold traditional Willow pattern with frosted background, border is turquoise and gold, $55.00 – 75.00. *Courtesy of Pam S. Donahue.*

Plate 336
Plate, Depression glass, 11½"d., unmarked, decorative salad–type plate, gold traditional Willow pattern with frosted background, border is a light purple and gold, $55.00 – 75.00. *Courtesy of Pam S. Donahue.*

Plate 337
Plate, Depression glass, 8½"d., bowl, Cambridge Glass Company, Cambridge, Ohio, c. 1902 – 1958, unmarked, green–filled etching on reverse side of bowl causes the traditional Willow pattern and border to appear reversed, gold trim, $75.00 – 95.00. *Courtesy of Pam S. Donahue.*

Plate 338
Plate, Depression glass, 10"d., unmarked, Cambridge Glass Company, Cambridge, Ohio, amber glass, gold traditional border etched on back appears to reverse the border, possibly used as a sandwich tray or for dainty desserts, $75.00 – 125.00+. *Courtesy of Pam S. Donahue.*

Plate 339
Plate, grill, 9¾"d., James Kent Ltd., Fenton, England, see Mark 38, evenly spaced on each side of the rim of the sectional divide are impressed circular areas, perhaps for salt; scalloped rim, $35.00 – 45.00. *Courtesy of David R. Harman, Jr.*

Plate 340
Plate, grill, 10½"d., unmarked, Japanese, note shape of sectional divider, $15.00 – 20.00. *Courtesy of David R. Harman, Jr.*

Plate 341

Plate 342

Plate 343

Plate 344

Plate 341

Plate, grill, 10½"d., note each compartment has a section of the traditional Willow pattern, $35.00 – 45.00. *Courtesy of David R. Harman, Jr.*

Plate 342

Plate, grill, 9½"d., Petrus Regout, Maestricht, Holland, see Mark 135, traditional Willow pattern altered a bit to fit into five sections of plate, perhaps used for sandwiches or relish, $35.00 – 55.00. *Author's Collection.*

Plate 343

Plate, grill, 10½"d., Japanese, see Mark 98, $15.00 – 18.00. *Courtesy of Paul and Bonnie Houck.*

Plate 344

Plate, grill, 10½"d., John Steventon & Sons, Ltd., Burslem, England, see Mark 65, c. 1923 – 1936, $15.00 – 20.00. *Courtesy of Paul and Bonnie Houck.*

Plate 345

Plate, grill, 10"d., Shenango China Company, New Castle, Pennsylvania, USA, see Mark 124, green Willow, traditional border, island scenes and building on far side of the bridge placed into the sections of the plate, used for relish or sandwiches, $25.00 – 35.00. *Author's Collection.*

Plate 346

Plate, hot water, 10½" d., 2"h., Ridgways, see Mark 56, traditional Willow border on ceramic bottom and spout, $250.00+. *Courtesy of David R. Harman, Jr.*

Plate 347

Plate, hot water, 10"d., unmarked, brass handles, stopper, and bottom, $175.00 – 200.00. *Courtesy of David R. Harman, Jr.*

Plate 345

Plate 346

Plate 347

Plate 348
Plate, serving platter, Two Temples II pattern, Butterfly border, multicolored, two handles, $65.00 – 85.00. *Courtesy of Pam S. Donahue.*

Plate 349
Plate, serving platter, Two Temples II pattern, Butterfly border, (note the large butterfly on the right handle), $75.00 – 95.00. *Courtesy of David R. Harman, Jr.*

Plate 350
Plate, serving platter, 10", Grimwades Ltd., Staffordshire, England, see Mark 28, traditional border, molded handles, $45.00 – 65.00. *Courtesy of David R. Harman, Jr.*

Plate 351
Plate, 5¼" handle to handle, Edge, Malkin & Co., England, see Mark 25, possibly used for condiments such as sauce or butter, perhaps a lid went with this piece, $35.00 – 55.00. *Courtesy of David R. Harman, Jr.*

Plate 348

Plate 349

Plate 350

Plate 351

Plate 352

Plate 353

Plate 354

Plate 355

Plate 352

Plate, 6"d., Booths, England, see Mark 12c, Booths pattern, Bow Knot border, $55.00 – 65.00. *Courtesy of David R. Harman, Jr.*

Plate 353

Plate, 7¼"d., Old Hall Earthenware Co. Ltd., England, see Mark 34, Mandarin pattern, Dagger or Fleur-de-lis border, $35.00 – 45.00. *Author's Collection.*

Plate 354

Plate, 6¼"d., black JAPAN mark, see Mark 86, teal colored Willow, hard to find, $20.00 – 35.00. *Author's Collection.*

Plate 355

Plate, 6" d., Japanese, traditional Willow pattern, bridge is missing, $15.00 – 25.00.

Plate 356
Plate, 6"d., unmarked, English, Two Temples I pattern, Butterfly border, note plate on left is slightly darker in color than one on right, $15.00 – 25.00 each. *Courtesy of David R. Harman, Jr.*

Plate 357
Plate, 7"d., Ridgways, English, see Mark 58, impressed with number 17, $35.00 – 45.00. *Courtesy of David R. Harman, Jr.*

Plate 358
Plate, 6"d., Barker Bros. Ltd., Longton, England, see Mark 8, gold trim between inner and outer border, $15.00 – 25.00. *Courtesy of David R. Harman, Jr.*

Plate 359
Plate, 8"d., Buffalo Pottery Co., see Mark 107, scalloped edges, $25.00 – 35.00. *Courtesy of David R. Harman, Jr.*

Plate 356

Plate 357

Plate 358

Plate 359

Plate 360

Plate 360
Plate, 9¾"d., The Royal China Company, see Mark 121, simple stamped traditional Willow pattern, Bridal Gold border pattern, $12.00 – 15.00. *Author's Collection.*

Plate 361
Plate, 9"d., Ridgways, England, see Mark 57, traditional Willow pattern and border, $35.00 – 45.00. *Courtesy of David R. Harman, Jr.*

Plate 362
Plate, 7¾"d., unmarked, English, pink Bow Knot border with Blue Willow traditional pattern medallions, $25.00 – 35.00. *Courtesy of David R. Harman, Jr.*

Plate 363
Plate, 6"d., Wood & Sons, England, see Mark 75, variant Willow center pattern, Bow Knot border, multicolored Willow, $65.00 – 75.00. *Courtesy of Pam S. Donahue.*

Plate 362

Plate 361

Plate 363

Plate 364

Plate 365

Plate 364
Plate, 10½"d., W.T. Copeland, England, see Mark 16, bone china plate, Temple–Landscape pattern in gold on a white background, gold border on a sea green/turquoise color, with butterflies, $50.00 – 75.00. *Courtesy of Pam S. Donahue.*

Plate 365
Plate, 10¼"d., Wedgwood, England, see Mark 73, standard (traditional) Willow pattern and border in gold on white background, $75.00 – 95.00. *Courtesy of Pam S. Donahue.*

Plate 366
Plate, 10¼"d., Wako China Co., Japan, see Mark 88, Willow pattern in a silver-blue color, no fence in foreground, $45.00 – 65.00. *Courtesy of Pam S. Donahue.*

Plate 367
Plate, 10½"d., W.T. Copeland, England, see Mark 16, mark is in red, Temple–Landscape center pattern in 24K gold on an ivory background, Butterfly border in 24K gold on a cobalt blue background, $75.00 – 100.00. *Courtesy of Eileen Callow.*

Plate 366

Plate 367

Plate 368
Plate, 9"d., Mason's, cobalt blue with gold Turner pattern, England, early 1900s, Scroll and Flower border, beautiful piece, $125.00+. *Courtesy of JWS.*

Plate 369
Plate, 8"d., G.L. Ashworth & Bros., Fenton, England, see Mark 7, Willow variant transfer pattern with overpainting in various shades, $5.00 – 10.00. *Author's Collection.*

Plate 370
Plate, 10"d., Wedgwood, England, see Mark 73, traditional Willow pattern, yellow transfer with overpainting, $75.00 – 100.00. *Courtesy of Pam S. Donahue.*

Plate 371
Plate, 7⅞"d., E.J.O. Bodley, England, c. 1875 – 1892, brown/rust Willow; $55.00 – 75.00. *Courtesy of Jeanne Berlew.*

Plate 368

Plate 369

Plate 370

Plate 371

— Photo Gallery —

Plate 372
Plate, 10½"d., unknown maker, Puerto Rico, USA, see Mark 137, $25.00 – 35.00. *Author's Collection.*

Plate 373
Plate, 11"d., Shenango China Co., see Mark 124, green–blue Willow, variant Willow pattern, Scroll and Flower border, $35.00 – 55.00. *Courtesy of Pam S. Donahue.*

Plate 374
Plate, 9"d., Japanese, see Mark 86, traditional Willow pattern in brown with color, $35.00 – 45.00.

Plate 375
Plate, 9"d., black Japan mark, see Mark 86, variant Willow pattern, note the two swan/goose-like birds, interesting piece, $35.00 – 45.00. *Courtesy of David R. Harman, Jr.*

Plate 372

Plate 373

Plate 374

Plate 375

Plate 376
Plate, 8"d., unmarked, Japanese, reticulated border with three geometrical designs, late 1900s, $15.00 – 25.00. *Courtesy of David R. Harman, Jr.*

Plate 377
Plate, pie, 10¼"d., Moriyama, Japan, see Mark 95, $75.00 – 100.00. *Courtesy of JWS.*

Plate 378
Plate, 9"d., Shenango China Company, New Castle, Pennsylvania, USA, see Mark 123, miniature circle Willow center pattern and inner border located at top of plate with an anchor above it on the rim. Anchor probably notes use by the Navy. Simple blue lines for borders, $35.00 – 50.00. *Courtesy of David R. Harman, Jr.*

Plate 375

Plate 376

Plate 377

Plate 378

Plate 380

Plate 379

Plate 381

Plate 379

Plate, 10"d., Hazel Atlas Glass Company, Clarksburg, West Virginia, USA, red Willow on Moderntone Platonite glass, standard (traditional) Willow pattern, red lines for border on rim, $25.00 – 45.00. *Courtesy of David R. Harman III.*

Plate 380

Plate, 9"d., Jackson China Company, Falls Creek, Pennsylvania, USA, see Mark 114, red Willow, standard (traditional) Willow circular pattern, no inner border, traditional border, $15.00 – 18.00. *Courtesy of David R. Harman III.*

Plate 381

Plate, 4"d., saucer, Bourne & Leigh, England, c. 1892 – 1939, see Mark 13, traditional Willow pattern, no border, $20.00 – 25.00. *Courtesy of David R. Harman, Jr.*

Plate 382

Plate, 4½"d., saucer, Made in Japan, see Mark 99, multicolored decal, late 1990s, price in 1997, $14.50. *Author's Collection.*

Plate 383

Plate, souvenir, 4"d., Japanese, see Mark 87, traditional Willow border, center design features a color-coded map of Cape Cod, Massachusetts, gold trim around rim and center pattern, $15.00 – 20.00. *Author's Collection.*

Plate 384

Plate, souvenir, Made in Brazil, see Mark 129, "Merry Christmas," Willow center pattern, gold birds in green border around rim, $25.00 – 35.00. *Author's Collection.*

Plate 385

Plate, octagonal shaped, paper label, "Oriental Trading," decorative use only, price in 1998, $11.99. *Courtesy of David R. Harman, Jr.*

Plate 386

Plate, 9¼"d., square shape, unmarked, multicolored traditional Willow decal, line border, molded, $45.00 – 55.00. *Courtesy of Pam S. Donahue.*

Plate 383

Plate 382

Plate 384

Plate 385

Plate 386

Plate 387

Plate 388

Plate 387
Plate, 6½" d., square shape, unmarked, English, scalloped corners, gold trim, $20.00 – 30.00. *Courtesy of David R. Harman, Jr.*

Plate 388
Plate, triangular side plate, 6" d., Burleigh, "Reg. Shape 733381," England, c. 1930+, $395.00 – 595.00+. *Courtesy of JWS.*

Plate 389
Platter, 21"x 10½", fish platter, William Alsager Adderley, see Mark 2, rare, traditional Willow pattern was applied lengthwise to best fill shape of platter, $525.00+. *Courtesy of Brenda Osmer.*

Plate 389

Plate 390
Platter, 11"l., English, c. 1883, Copeland, Mandarin pattern, gold and cobalt border. $475.00 – 500.00+. *Courtesy of JWS.*

Plate 391
Platter, 8½" x 11½", Canonsburg Pottery Co., Canonsburg, Pennsylvania, see Mark 108, Two Temples II reversed pattern, simple rubber stamp, note border pattern, $20.00 – 35.00. *Author's Collection.*

Plate 392
Platter, 13¼"d., unmarked, American, also shown with attached metal carrier handle, $20.00 – 30.00. *Courtesy of Paul and Bonnie Houck.*

Plate 390

Plate 391

Plate 392

Plate 392

Plate 393

Plate 394

Plate 393

Platter, 10"x 12", Edwin M. Knowles, Roselace shape, molded border shape, rose colored glaze, multicolored decal, traditional Willow pattern, missing birds, $35.00 – 50.00. *Courtesy of William and Vitalia Hodgetts.*

Plate 394

Platter, 9"d., Booths, Tunstall, England, see Mark 12c, oval shape, pink/red, almost an orange colored Willow, Booths pattern, Bow Knot border, $75.00 – 95.00. *Courtesy of Pam S. Donahue.*

Plate 395

Platter, 7¼"d., Jackson China Company, Falls Creek, Pennsylvania, USA, see Mark 113, red Willow, standard (traditional) Willow pattern in a circular shape, no inner border, traditional outer border, $15.00 – 18.00. *Courtesy of David R. Harman III.*

Plate 396

Platter, 11¾"d., The Paden City Pottery Company, Paden City, West Virginia, USA, see Mark 119, impressed standard (traditional) Willow pattern, Butterfly border (ordinarily associated with Two Temples II outer border), coated with a blue glaze, $25.00 – 35.00. *Courtesy of David R. Harman, Jr.*

Plate 395

Plate 396

Plate 397

Plate 398

Plate 397
Platter, 9½"d., Brown and Steventon Ltd., England, see Mark 10, (note the inner border seems stretched at the ends to fit the oval shape) $55.00 – 65.00. *Courtesy of David R. Harman, Jr.*

Plate 398
Platter, 12"d., House of Blue Willow, Made in Japan, see Mark 84, $55.00 – 65.00. *Courtesy of David R. Harman, Jr.*

Plate 399
Platter, 10" x 8", unmarked, Limoges China Company, Sebring, Ohio, USA, c. 1924, Two Temples II pattern, decal, blue line border with gold loop design, $45.00 – 55.00. *Courtesy of William and Vitalia Hodgetts.*

Plate 399

Plate 400

Plate 401

Plate 402

Plate 403

Plate 400

Platter, 18½"d., Wade Heath & Co. Ltd., c. 1927 – present, England, see Mark 69, circular unknown variant Willow pattern, Willow motifs (Willow tree, boats, oriental landscape) in the white background area, inner border, variant Butterfly border, four handles, gold trim, $45.00 – 55.00. *Courtesy of David R. Harman, Jr.*

Plate 401

Platter, 12½"d., Made in England for L. Bamberger & Co., see Mark 81, scalloped edge, $75.00 – 100.00. *Courtesy of David R. Harman, Jr.*

Plate 402

Platter, 12½" x 10", Made in England, see Mark 42, $225.00. *Courtesy of David R. Harman, Jr.*

Plate 403

Platter, 12" x 9½", Brown & Steventon Ltd., England, c. 1903 – 1923, see Mark 10, $225.00 – 275.00. *Courtesy of David R. Harman, Jr.*

Plate 404

Platter, 10½"d., oval shape, Jackson China Company, see Mark 113, "Kow Sun" printed above circular red pattern $25.00 – 35.00. *Author's Collection.*

Plate 405

Platter, 10" x 8", Brittania Pottery Co. Ltd., Glasgow, Scotland, see Mark 140, purple traditional Willow pattern, $150.00 – 175.00. *Courtesy of Brenda Osmer.*

Plate 404

Plate 405

Plate 406

Plate 407

Plate 406
Platter, 12", round shape, traditional Willow pattern decal, multicolored Willow, simple orange color border, $35.00 – 55.00. *Courtesy of William and Vitalia Hodgetts.*

Plate 407
Platter, 12"d., round shape, Noritake, Japan, see Mark 85, beautifully painted pattern with various colors including gold, red, and blue, on a turquoise background, rust colored luster border, $45.00 – 55.00. *Author's Collection.*

Plate 408
Potpourri keeper, missing lid, reticulated, 5"h., unmarked, English, c. 1800, pearlware, early vase, variant Butterfly border on base, interior, and exterior of vase opening, $1,000.00 – 1,200.00. *Courtesy of Loren Zeller.*

Plate 409
Pudding mold, 3½"h., 4½"d., unmarked, English, Two Temples II pattern, Pictorial border, multicolored Willow, $95.00 – 110.00. *Courtesy of William and Vitalia Hodgetts.*

Plate 408

Plate 409

Plate 410

Plate 411

Plate 412

Plate 413

Plate 410

Pudding mold, 4½"h, unmarked, English, $75.00 – 85.00. *Courtesy of David R. Harman, Jr.*

Plate 411

Relish, 5½"h., with metal lid and attached fork, Lancaster & Sandland Ltd., Hanley, England, see Mark 41, hand-painted Willow variant pattern, $60.00 – 75.00. *Courtesy of Pam S. Donahue.*

Plate 412

Relish, 8"d., fish finial, unmarked, Japanese, three divided sections, gold trim on edges, $75.00 – 125.00. *Courtesy of Pam S. Donahue.*

Plate 413

Relish, 9½"d., Buffalo China, see Mark 101, note center pattern placed lengthwise to fill space, $55.00 – 65.00. *Courtesy of David R. Harman, Jr.*

Plate 414

Plate 414

Plate 414
Relish, 7¾"d., Walker China, Bedford, Ohio, see Mark 127, dish has scalloped edge and ridges, $65.00 – 75.00. *Courtesy of David R. Harman, Jr.*

Plate 415
Relish, 8"d., Old Hall Earthenware Co. Ltd., England, see Mark 34, $75.00 – 85.00. *Courtesy of David R. Harman, Jr.*

Plate 416
Salad fork and spoon, unmarked, Japanese, green Willow pattern, ceramic handles, with wooden fork or spoon ends, $15.00 – 25.00. *Courtesy of Pam S. Donahue.*

Plate 417
Salad fork and spoon, unmarked, Japanese, ceramic handles, with wooden fork and spoon ends, $15.00 – 25.00. *Courtesy of Pam S. Donahue.*

Plate 415

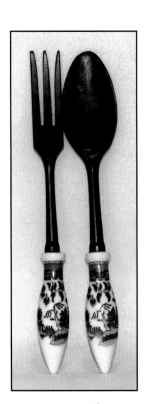

Plate 416

Plate 417

Plate 418

Plate 419

Plate 420

Plate 421

Plate 418
Box, 6½"h., unmarked, wooden lid, printed "Salt," variant Willow pattern decal, $175.00 – 200.00. *Courtesy of Pam S. Donahue.*

Plate 419
Salt box, 4½" x 5", unmarked, Japanese, wooden lid, hole for hanging on wall, $250.00 – 300.00. *Courtesy of Pam S. Donahue.*

Plate 420
Salt dips, 2"h., unmarked, English, Mandarin pattern, interior Dagger or Fleur–de–lis border, beautiful craftsmanship, footed bases, $100.00 – 125.00 each. *Courtesy of David R. Harman, Jr.*

Plate 421
Salt shaker and pepper mill, 3"h., George S. Thompson Corporation, Olde Thompson, USA, see Mark 110, (Flintridge China Company made the china case, see Mark 109) metal top and grinder (pepper only), shown in original box, $75.00 – 100.00 set. *Author's Collection.*

Plate 422

Plate 423

Plate 424

Plate 422

Salt shaker and pepper mill, 3"h., George S. Thompson Corporation, Olde Thompson, USA, see Mark 110 (Flintridge China Company made the china case, see Mark 109), white colored metal lids and grinder (pepper only), with gold trim, $85.00 – 120.00 set. *Courtesy of Pam S. Donahue.*

Plate 423

Salt shaker and pepper mill, 3"h., George S. Thompson Corporation, Olde Thompson, Monterey Park (pepper mill), South Pasadena, California, USA (salt), see Mark 110 (Flintridge China Company made the china case, see Mark 109) standard (traditional) Willow pattern in red, simplified border, $75.00 – 85.00 set. *Courtesy of David R. Harman III.*

Plate 424

Salt and pepper shakers, various shapes and sizes, Japanese, back row: $20.00 – 35.00 pair, front row: left, $35.00 – 45.00 pair, right, 20.00 – 35.00 pair. *Author's Collection.*

Plate 425

Salt and pepper, 3½"h., tray, 5¾"l., Japanese, salt/pepper, bulbous shape, shakers and tray are both marked in blue, Made in Japan, see Mark 99, probably not an original set, $30.00 – 35.00 set, $10.00 – 12.00 for shakers. *Courtesy of David R. Harman, Jr.*

Plate 426

Salt and pepper, with handles, Royal China Company, Sebring, Ohio, USA, pink Willow, standard (traditional) Willow pattern, no border, salt/pepper holes are in the shapes of an "S" and a "P," $20.00 – 25.00 set. *Courtesy of David R. Harman III.*

Plate 427

Salt and pepper, 4"h., tray, 6"l., marked in black, ESD Japan, see Mark 93, shakers unmarked, Japanese, probably not an original set, $35.00 – 40.00 for shakers, $10.00 – 12.00 for tray. *Courtesy of David R. Harman, Jr.*

Plate 425

Plate 427

Plate 426

Plate 428

Plate 429

Plate 428
Salt and pepper, 2½"h., red/gold paper label, "Imports Enesco Japan," Simplified Willow pattern, gold trim, $25.00 – 35.00. *Author's Collection.*

Plate 429
Salt shaker, 5½"h., English "Bobby" salt shaker, very rare, c. 1880 – 1890, $275.00 – 350.00+. *Courtesy of Loren Zeller.*

Plate 430
Shaving mug, unmarked, variant Willow pattern decal, dainty blue flower decals around the border and near opening for shaving brush. This particular piece has a lot of heavy crazing, $50.00 – 75.00. *Courtesy of David R. Harman, Jr.*

Plate 431
Sherbet, 3½"h., Made in Japan, see Mark 99, Two Temples II Pattern, Butterfly border, blue border on base, $40.00 – 45.00. *Courtesy of David R. Harman, Jr.*

Plate 430

Plate 431

— *Photo Gallery* —

Plate 432
Sherbet, 2¼"h., 3½"d., Shenango China Company, New Castle, Pennsylvania, see Mark 124, traditional center pattern, traditional border on interior, $30.00 – 35.00. *Courtesy of David R. Harman, Jr.*

Plate 433
Sherbets, 3¼"h., Hazel Atlas Glass Company, Clarksville, West Virginia, USA, see Mark 128, c. late 1930s – 1956, Moderntone Platonite, opaque white glass with red traditional Willow pattern, simple red line border, $25.00 – 30.00 each. *Courtesy of Pam S. Donahue.*

Plate 434
Soap, 2⅞ oz., Willow Beauty Soap, A Peter Lunt Product, England, "Milk and Almond Oil," $ND. *Courtesy of JWS.*

Plate 435
Soap dish, 5½"l., Burgess & Leigh, see Mark 14, Burleigh center pattern, Floral variant border, center has "ridges" for soap, $25.00 – 35.00. *Courtesy of David R. Harman, Jr.*

Plate 432

Plate 433

Plate 434

Plate 435

Plate 436

Plate 436

Plate 436
Spice racks, 4½"h., book shaped shakers with two ceramic drawers, hanging wooden racks, $175.00 – 250.00 each. *Author's Collection.*

Plate 437
Spice rack, 2½"h., shakers, 7"h., 6½"w., paper label, black/gold JAPAN, each shaker has a knob in the top center with a spice name above the knob, hanging wooden rack, $150.00 – 200.00. *Courtesy of David R. Harman Jr.*

Plate 438
Spoon rest, 9"l., impressed "JAPAN" on back, triple spoon rest, hole for hanging, center reads "SPOON REST" in light black, Willow motifs in each spoon rest, $45.00 – 50.00. *Courtesy of David R. Harman, Jr.*

Plate 439
Spoon rest, 9"l., impressed "JAPAN" on back, double spoon rest, hole for hanging, center reads "SPOON REST" in black, Willow motifs in each spoon rest, $35.00 – 45.00. *Courtesy of David R. Harman, Jr.*

Plate 440
Spoon rest, unmarked, Japanese, double spoon rest, center reads "SPOONER" in black, hole for hanging, Willow motifs in each spoon rest, $25.00 – 35.00.

Plate 441
Spoon rest, unmarked, Japanese, top reads "SPOON REST" in blue, triple spoon rest, standard Willow features, $15.00 – 25.00. *Author's Collection.*

Plate 437

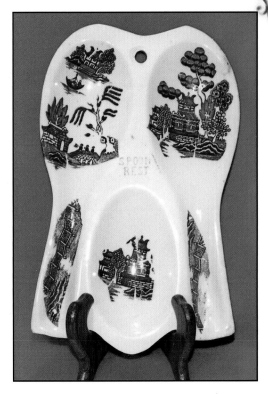

Plate 438

Plate 439

Plate 440

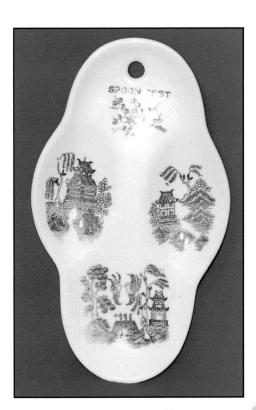

Plate 441

Plate 442

Plate 443

Plate 443

Plate 444

Plate 445

Plate 446

Plate 442
Sugar barrel, or possibly a biscuit barrel, 5¼"h., unmarked, English, late twentieth century, metal lid and handle, $150.00 – 200.00. *Courtesy of JWS.*

Plate 443
Sugar bowl or cuber, 7¼"h., unmarked, English, lovely piece, fancy claw-like molded handles, decorative finial, standard (traditional) Willow pattern, no birds, traditional border, may have been used for sugar cubes, $125.00 – 150.00. *Courtesy of David R. Harman, Jr.*

Plate 444
Sugar bowl or cuber, unmarked, English, lid has open handle, standard (traditional) Willow pattern, traditional border, may have been used for sugar cubes, $125.00 – 150.00. *Courtesy of David R. Harman, Jr.*

Plate 445
Sugar bowl, 5¼"h., Moriyama, Japan, see Mark 95, beautiful, $50.00 – 75.00. *Courtesy of David R. Harman, Jr.*

Plate 446
Sugar bowl, 4"h., Lancaster & Sandland, Ltd., Hanley, England, c. 1949+, hand-painted variant Willow pattern, metal lid with opening for spoon, four feet, see Mark 41, $35.00 – 50.00. *Author's Collection.*

Plate 447
Sugar bowl, 5¼"h., William Adams & Sons, see Mark 3, lovely rosebud finial, $55.00 – 75.00. *Courtesy of David R. Harman, Jr.*

Plate 448
Sugar bowl, 5¼"h., Buffalo Pottery, Buffalo, New York, 1911, see Mark 104, standard (traditional) Willow pattern, traditional border, $100.00 – 150.00. *Courtesy of David R. Harman, Jr.*

Plate 447

Plate 448

Plate 449

Plate 450

Plate 451

Plate 449
Sugar and creamer, 5¼"h. each, Japanese, see Mark 96, Nihon Koshitsu Toki Co. interpretation of the Booth pattern, Bow Knot border, $45.00 – 65.00. *Courtesy of David R. Harman, Jr.*

Plate 450
Sugar bowl, open (no lid), 3"d., and creamer, 3"h., Booths, England, see Mark 12, Booths pattern, Bow Knot border, possibly individual set or child's set, see Marks 12a and 12b, $125.00 – 145.00 set. *Courtesy of David R. Harman, Jr.*

Plate 451
Sugar bowl, 5"h. to knob, and creamer, 3½"h., black JAPAN mark, demitasse size, $35.00 – 45.00 set. *Courtesy of David R. Harman, Jr.*

Plate 452
Sugar bowl, 4"h. to knob, creamer, 3"h., and tray, 7¼" l., unmarked, Japanese, tray has traditional border, possibly not original set, $45.00 – 55.00 set. *Courtesy of David R. Harman, Jr.*

Plate 453
Sugar bowl, 4"h., and creamer, 3¾"h., unmarked, Homer Laughlin China Company, hollowware, unmarked, $25.00 – 45.00. *Author's Collection.*

Plate 454
Sugar bowl, 4"h., and creamer, 3¼"h., Societe Ceramique, Maestricht, Holland, see Mark 136, fish roe border (a commonly seen trait of this company), standard (traditional) Willow pattern, $35.00 – 55.00. *Courtesy of David R. Harman, Jr.*

Plate 452

Plate 453

Plate 454

Plate 455

Plate 456

Plate 457

Plate 458

Plate 455
Sugar bowls, Ridgways, England, see Marks 57 and 59, embossed bamboo leaves on handles, beautiful, $175.00 – 225.00 set. *Courtesy of David R. Harman, Jr.*

Plate 456
Sugar bowl, 5½"d., Walker China Company, USA, see Mark 127, standard (traditional) Willow pattern, no border, hinged metal lid, slot for spoon, $55.00 – 70.00. *Courtesy of Pam S. Donahue.*

Plate 457
Sugar bowl, 4½"d., Walker China Company, USA, see Mark 127a, Two Temples II pattern, no border, hinged metal lid, slot for spoon, $65.00 – 75.00. *Courtesy of Pam S. Donahue.*

Plate 458
Sugar, 2½"h., open, (no lid), Lancaster & Sandland, Ltd., Hanley, England, c. 1949+, see Mark 41, $45.00 – 55.00. *Author's Collection.*

Plate 459

Plate 459
Sugar, 4¼" to knob, Lancaster & Sandland, Ltd., Hanley, England, c. 1949+, see Mark 41, metal lid and handle, on metal rim and inside of lid is stamped: "Yeoman Plate E.P.N.S. Made in England," $55.00 – 75.00. *Author's Collection.*

Plate 460
Supper tray, four dishes (12"l. x 6"w. x 4½"h.) and four covers, each marked with a small dark blue crown, unknown English maker, Bridgeless Willow pattern, beautiful; $2,500.00+. *Courtesy of Glenn and Rosemary Gibbs.*

Plate 461
Tea caddy, with lid, 5¼"h., 3½" x 2", backstamp: Nankin, $325.00 – 475.00. *Courtesy of Glenn and Rosemary Gibbs.*

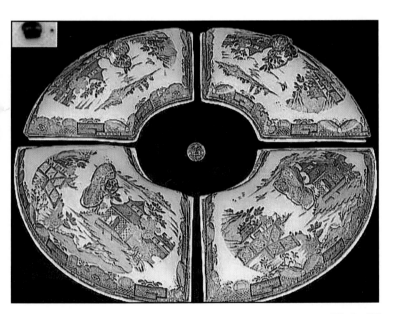

Plate 460

Plate 461

Plate 462

Plate 463

Plate 464

Plate 464

Plate 462
Tea canister, 4½"h., chrome, missing lid, unmarked, English, etched Willow pattern, word "tea" is on each canister, $50.00 – 75.00 each. *Courtesy of Pam S. Donahue.*

Plate 463
Tea canister, 4½"h., missing lid, chrome, unmarked, English, etched Willow pattern, back view of Plate 462, $45.00 – 50.00. *Courtesy of Pam S. Donahue.*

Plate 464
Tea canisters, 4½"h., chrome, unmarked, English, etched Willow pattern, word "tea" is on each canister, $50.00 – 75.00 each. *Courtesy of Pam S. Donahue.*

Plate 465
Tea set, teapot, 6"h., sugar, 3¾"h., creamer, 3"h., Allerton, England, see Mark 4, beautiful set, note birds on teapot spout, $350.00 – 400.00 set. *Courtesy of Jeanne Berlew.*

Plate 466
Tea set, Copeland Spode, c. 1880, set includes a serving tray with beautifully crafted handles, a teapot, open sugar and creamer, and two cups/saucers, note handle design on teapot and cups, $2,500.00+ set. *Courtesy of Loren Zeller.*

Plate 465

Plate 466

Plate 467

Plate 467

Plate 467
Tea set, two teapots, teacups/saucers, creamer/sugar, standard (traditional) Willow pattern, "We'll Take a Cup O'kindness Yet for Days O' Auld Lang Syne" on borders of teapots, creamer, and sugar and on interior of cups/saucers, lion-shaped finials on teapots and sugar, also known as "Burns Willow," teapot and sugar are angular shaped, hexagonal, the scalloped shaped serving tray has standard (traditional) Willow pattern with traditional borders and gold trim, rare and exquisite set, see Marks 16 and 18. Teapots, $300.00 – 350.00 each; creamer/sugar, $275.00 – 300.00 set; teacups/saucers, $100.00 – 125.00 each; serving tray, $500.00+. *Courtesy of Brenda Osmer.*

Plate 468
Teapot (Cosy), 8"h., sugar and creamer stack on the teapot then the lid is placed atop the creamer. Marked JAPAN, see Mark 86, $150.00 – 200.00. *Courtesy of David R. Harman, Jr.*

Plate 469
Teapot (Cosy), stackable creamer/sugar, 1½"h., unmarked, $15.00 – 25.00 each. *Courtesy of Paul and Bonnie Houck.*

Plate 470
Tea (Cosy) Pot, 8½" h, stackable creamer/sugar, Moriyama, Japan, see Mark 95, $175.00 – 225.00. *Courtesy of Joette Hightower.*

Plate 468

Plate 469

Plate 470

Plate 471

Teapot, 7¾"h., impressed "Copeland," red Mandarin pattern, Dagger or Fleur-de-lis border, with kettle handle, $275.00 – 350.00. *Courtesy of JWS.*

Plate 472

Teapot, 6¾"h., unmarked, English, early nineteenth century, Two Temples I pattern, gold finial and trim, fluted design, beautiful, $275.00 – 325.00. *Courtesy of JWS.*

Plate 473

Teapot, 6"h., marked "Semi–China," possibly Ridgways, see Mark 56, Two Temples II reversed pattern, Butterfly border, note the bamboo leaf design on handles with gold trim accenting the bamboo design, $375.00+. *Courtesy of JWS.*

Plate 474

Teapot, 8"h., large, 3-quart, unmarked, c. 1900s. Due to the size of this teapot a handle was added to the front above the spout to help the pourer hold the weight of the filled teapot. $425.00 – 525.00. *Courtesy of Loren Zeller.*

Plate 471

Plate 472

Plate 473

Plate 474

Plate 475

Plate 476

Plate 475
Teapot, 9"h., self–pouring, Doulton, c. 1890. Metal lid is pumped, the hot water is forced through the tea leaves, then comes out the spout. In the base is an area for the tea leaves with perforated holes. Cobalt blue spout and handles with gold accents, traditional Willow pattern, $575.00+. *Courtesy of Loren Zeller.*

Plate 476
Teapot, square or cube shape, Grimwades, Ltd., intriguing and unusual shape, $325.00 – 425.00. *Courtesy of William and Vitalia Hodgetts.*

Plate 477
Teapot, 9½"l., 7"h., Arthur Wood, England, see Mark 74a, scalloped footed bottom, Willow pattern also on lid, $175.00 – 225.00. *Courtesy of Brenda Osmer.*

Plate 477

Plate 478

Plate 479

Plate 480

Plate 481

Plate 482

Plate 483

Plate 484

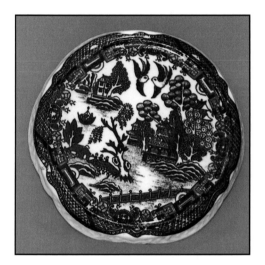

Plate 484

Plate 485

Plate 478
Teapot, 6½"h., unmarked, English, rosebud finial, standard (traditional) Willow pattern, no border, $55.00 – 75.00. *Courtesy of David R. Harman, Jr.*

Plate 479
Teapot, Sadler, England, see Mark 63, fluted, gold trim and finial, $75.00 – 100.00. *Courtesy of David R. Harman, Jr.*

Plate 480
Teapot, 5½"h., black JAPAN mark, standard (traditional) Willow pattern, traditional border, spout has Willow motifs, $45.00 – 65.00. *Courtesy of David R. Harman, Jr.*

Plate 481
Teapot, 7"h., barrel shaped, unmarked, Japanese, Willow motifs on spout, $75.00 – 100.00. *Courtesy of David R. Harman, Jr.*

Plate 482
Teapot, 6"h., House of Blue Willow, Japanese, see Mark 84, standard (traditional) Willow, traditional Willow border, Willow motifs on spout and lid, $50.00 – 75.00. *Courtesy of David R. Harman, Jr.*

Plate 483
Teapot, 6"h., unmarked, Japanese, standard (traditional) Willow, traditional Willow border, Willow motifs on spout and lid, $50.00 – 75.00. *Courtesy of David R. Harman, Jr.*

Plate 484
Teapot, 6½"h., and trivet, 6½"d., both marked in blue, Made in Japan, see Mark 99, standard (traditional) Willow pattern, traditional border, (reversed on teapot) motifs on lid, $100.00 – 125.00 set. *Courtesy of David R. Harman, Jr.*

Plate 485
Teapot, 5½"h., unmarked, Homer Laughlin China Company, East Liverpool, Ohio, USA, handle has a diamond design, standard (traditional) Willow pattern, traditional Willow border is reversed, $65.00 – 85.00. *Courtesy of David R. Harman, Jr.*

Plate 486

Plate 487

Plate 488

Plate 489

Plate 486
Teapot, 6½"h., unmarked, Japanese, standard (traditional) Willow pattern, traditional Willow border, standard Willow pattern on lid and no border, $50.00 – 75.00. *Courtesy of David R. Harman, Jr.*

Plate 487
Teapot, 5½"h., Ashworth Bros., England, see Mark 6, Two Temples II reversed pattern and variant border, shades of teal, $95.00 – 125.00. *Courtesy of Pam S. Donahue.*

Plate 488
Teapot, 5"h., Gibson & Sons, Burslem, England, c. 1950+, Mandarin pattern on black background, $175.00 – 200.00. *Courtesy of Pam S. Donahue.*

Plate 489
Teapot, 10" handle to handle, unmarked by Royal China Co., Sebring, Ohio, USA. Note pattern on spout, no design on handle, $45.00 – 75.00. *Courtesy of Paul and Bonnie Houck.*

Plate 490
Teapot, Churchhill, England, see Mark 20, $35.00 – 45.00. *Courtesy of Gary and Sandy Osenbaugh.*

Plate 491
Teapot, 9¼" h., Moriyama, Japan, see Mark 95, $275.00 – 300.00. *Courtesy of Joette Hightower.*

Plate 490

Plate 491

Plate 492

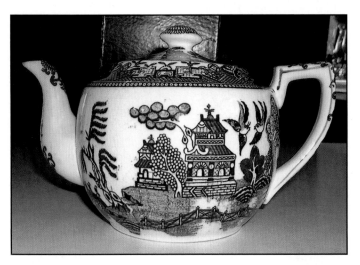

Plate 493

Plate 492
Teapot, 9"h., Moriyama, Japan, see Mark 95, $275.00 – 300.00. *Courtesy of Joette Hightower.*

Plate 493
Teapot, 10¼"h., Moriyama, Japan, see Mark 95, $275.00 – 300.00. *Courtesy of Joette Hightower.*

Plate 494
Teapot, 9¼"h., Moriyama, Japan, see Mark 95, red Willow, decorative handle and base have red trim, $300.00 – 350.00. *Courtesy of Joette Hightower.*

Plate 495
Teapot, 6½"h., Moriyama, Japan, see Mark 95, interesting lid, holds one cup, $125.00 – 150.00. *Courtesy of Joette Hightower.*

Plate 496
Tea bags, 25 count, in wooden box, 5¼"h., Fortunes Green Tea, features a teacup with Willow pattern, $5.00 – 10.00. *Courtesy of Paul and Bonnie Houck.*

Plate 497
Tea strainer, unmarked, Japanese, modern, holes to allow tea to drain, handle and spout pour out the excess strained tea, $15.00 – 25.00.

Plate 498
Tea kettle, 9¼"h. to top of handle, $30.00 – 45.00. *Courtesy of Pam S. Donahue.*

Plate 499
Tea kettle, 9" h. to top of handle, $30.00 – 45.00. *Courtesy of Pam S. Donahue.*

Plate 500
Tea kettles, 8"h. and 9½"h., $30.00 – 45.00. *Courtesy of Pam S. Donahue.*

Plate 494

Plate 495

Plate 497

Plate 496

Plate 498

Plate 499

Plate 500

Plate 501

Plate 502

Plate 501

Tea kettle, 5"h. to top of handle, aluminum, Swan Brand, England, marked "Swan Willow," c. 1970, see Mark 67, $50.00 – 75.00. *Author's Collection.*

Plate 502

Tea kettle, 3"h., missing lid, aluminum, made by N.C.U. Ltd., England, marked "Sona Ware," The Aluminium (misspelled) Works, Stratford–on–Avon, England, handle is riveted onto kettle body, standard Willow pattern, no border, $ND. *Author's Collection.*

Plate 503

Tier server, 10"h., 9"d. bottom plate, 7"d. top plate, Homer Laughlin China Company, USA, $45.00 – 75.00. *Courtesy of Paul and Bonnie Houck.*

Plate 504

Tile, 6", square, unmarked, English, standard (traditional) Willow pattern and border, $75.00 – 85.00. *Courtesy of JWS.*

Plate 505

Tile, 5⅞", square, marked England, standard (traditional) Willow pattern on back, interesting border, $75.00 – 85.00. *Courtesy of Brenda Osmer.*

Plate 506

Tile, 6", square, Soriano Ceramics, also may be a trivet, $45.00 – 50.00. *Courtesy of David R. Harman, Jr.*

Plate 507

Tins, set of three, unmarked, standard (traditional) Willow pattern and border on lids and outsides of tins, $15.00 – 25.00 set. *Author's Collection.*

Plate 503

Plate 504

Plate 505

Plate 506

Plate 507

Plate 508

Plate 509

Plate 508

Tin, 2"h., paper label, Keller-Charles of Philadelphia, Made in China, Willow pattern with a sleeping cat on top, $5.00 – 15.00. *Courtesy of Paul and Bonnie Houck.*

Plate 509

Tip plate, 5"d., marked Gien France, see Mark 131, advertisement for "Schweppes Bitter Lemon," standard (traditional) Willow pattern is reversed, $75.00 – 95.00. *Courtesy of David R. Harman, Jr.*

Plate 510

Tip plate, 4½"d., Made in England, see Mark 42, impressed "/7/34," advertisement for "Schweppes Devonshire Cider," standard (traditional) Willow pattern, partial traditional border with fish roe, $75.00 – 100.00. *Courtesy of David R. Harman, Jr.*

Plate 511

Tip plate, 4½" d., Made in France, see Mark 132, advertisement for "Schweppes Tonic Water," standard (traditional) Willow pattern, partial traditional border with fish roe, brown Willow, $75.00 – 110.00. *Courtesy of David R. Harman, Jr.*

Plate 510

Plate 511

— *Photo Gallery* —

Plate 512
Tip plate, 4½"d., Made in England, advertisement for "Schweppes Indian Tonic," standard (traditional) Willow pattern is reversed, $75.00 – 95.00. *Courtesy of David R. Harman, Jr.*

Plate 513
Tip tray, 6¼", unmarked, English, "The Antiquary" Old Scotch Whisky, reads "At last I found it," enamel ware tin, traditional Willow border, $125.00 – 145.00. *Courtesy of JWS.*

Plate 514
Toaster covers, 13"d., 11¼"d., and 11"d., each features repeated Willow pattern in material, $25.00 – 35.00 each. *Courtesy of Pam S. Donahue.*

Plate 514

Plate 512

Plate 514

Plate 513

Plate 514

Plate 515

Plate 516

Plate 517

Plate 518

Plate 519

Plate 520

Plate 515

Toby jugs 2¾"h., perfume bottle, 2¼"h., Toby's mark has fish mark, perfume bottle, hexagon shape, marked #RN80260, silverplated lid, Toby jugs, $525.00 each; perfume bottle, $375.00. *Courtesy of Eileen Callow.*

Plate 516

Toby jugs, left to right: 4½"h., "snuff taker," $1,300.00; 8"h., marked "Sampson Smith," c. 1851 – 1890, $1,500.00 – 1,800.00; 6"h, hat in front, $1,250.00 – 1,300.00. All three are attributed to Sampson Smith, Longton, England, 1851 – 1890, Willow pattern on hats and jackets, fine examples. *Courtesy of Loren Zeller.*

Plate 517

Toby Jugs, left: 6"h., William Kent, England, see Mark 40, c. late nineteenth century; right: 5¾"h., unmarked, English; standard (traditional) Willow pattern on jackets. $1,000.00 – 1,200.00+ each. *Courtesy of Jeanne Berlew.*

Plate 518

Toby jug, 5¾"h., marked 68, standard (traditional) Willow pattern on jacket, traditional border on hat and base, handle on side, purchased in late 1990s at Lousie's Old Things, Kutztown, PA, specially made for them), original price $35.00 in late 1990s. *Author's Collection.*

Plate 519

Toothbrush cover, unmarked, English, metal lid, for the bristle end of a toothbrush, $125.00 – 150.00. *Courtesy of Pam S. Donahue.*

Plate 520

Toothpick holder, 2"h., unmarked, Japanese, $25.00 – 45.00. *Courtesy of David R. Harman, Jr.*

Plate 521

Trivet, 11"l., 6½"d., square shape, unmarked, American, handle with hole for hanging, $35.00 – 45.00. *Courtesy of Paul and Bonnie Houck.*

Plate 521

Plate 522

Plate 522

Plate 523

Plate 522
Trays, 22"d. and 14"d., (also available in 11"d., 7"d., and 4½"d.), unmarked, English, brass trays in various sizes, etched Willow pattern, $75.00 – 125.00 each. *Courtesy of Pam S. Donahue and Arlene Coleman.*

Plate 523
Tumbler, 3¾"h., Burgess & Leigh, see Mark 14, Burleigh pattern, gold trim, no border, $45.00 – 65.00. *Courtesy of David R. Harman, Jr.*

Plate 524
Tumblers, 3¼" h., unmarked, Japanese, each tumbler shows Willow pattern, $25.00 – 30.00 each. *Courtesy of David R. Harman, Jr.*

Plate 525
Trowel, 5" l., unmarked, English, used with cheese or butter spreads, Two Temples I pattern, no border, $125.00 – 150.00. *Courtesy of David R. Harman, Jr.*

Plate 526
Tureen, 8"h., 12½"l., Ridgways, England, c. 1920s, Gaudy Willow, probably used for soup, beautiful cobalt blue handles and finial, $775.00 – 800.00. *Courtesy of JWS.*

Plate 524

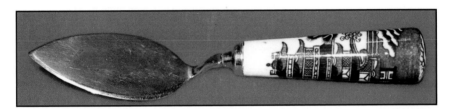

Plate 525

Plate 526

Plate 527

Plate 528

Plate 529

Plate 530

Plate 527
Tureen, 8½"h., 12"l., unknown English mark, see Mark 78, interesting finial and shape of lid, slot for ladle, $600.00 – 800.00. *Courtesy of Pam S. Donahue.*

Plate, 528
Tureen, 7½"h., 12½"l., 8½"w., Ridgways, England, see Mark 58, $800.00 – 1,000.00. *Courtesy of David R. Harman, Jr.*

Plate 529
Tureen, 8"h., 10"d., unmarked, English, $500.00 – 600.00. *Courtesy of David R. Harman, Jr.*

Plate 530
Tureen, 16½"l. handle to handle, 10"w. to knob, Johnson Bros., England, see Mark 36, $275.00 – 300.00. *Courtesy of David R. Harman, Jr.*

Plate 531
Tureen, electric, 12"l., 8"h., Japanese, red Willow, ladle has border on handle, $175.00 – 300.00. *Courtesy of David R. Harman III.*

Plate 532
Tureen, 14"w., 10"h., Mason's, England, see Mark 45, ironstone tureen with underplate, lid, ladle, beautiful Willow pattern arrangement, no birds, Scroll and Flower border, c. 1891 – 1910 (also seen in red Willow), $495.00 – 675.00. *Courtesy of Jeanne Berlew.*

Plate 533
Tureen, 6"h., unmarked, English, shell-shaped finial, footed base has Bow Knot border, tureen bowl/lid has standard (traditional) Willow pattern and border, $275.00 – 325.00. *Courtesy of David R. Harman, Jr.*

Plate 534
Tureen, 10" x 6", unmarked, Japanese, scalloped footed base, matching ladle, tray has traditional border, $175.00 – 225.00. *Courtesy of David R. Harman, Jr.*

Plate 531

Plate 532

Plate 533

Plate 534

Plate 536

Plate 535

Plate 535
Tureen, unmarked, unknown maker, modern, $100.00 – 125.00. *Courtesy of Paul and Bonnie Houck.*

Plate 536
Tureen, sauce, unmarked, English, interior pattern, $175.00 – 200.00. *Courtesy of David R. Harman, Jr.*

Plate 537
Tureen, sauce, Alfred Meakin, England, see Mark 47, (tray), lid and tureen rim have same shape, footed square base, $125.00 – 150.00. *Courtesy of David R. Harman, Jr.*

Plate 536

Plate 537

Plate 539

Plate 539

Plate 538

Plate 539

Plate 538
Umbrella stand, 18"h., 8½"w., unmarked, Japanese, c. 1970s, $75.00 – 125.00. *Courtesy of Brenda Osmer.*

Plate 539
Vaporizer, 7¼"h., Wood & Sons, England, c. 1910, base and insert have patent numbering, also marked "cosy" pot, pitcher would be filled with steaming hot water, medical powders or herbs would be placed into the removable lid insert, then the steam would be inhaled. $375.00 – 500.00. *Courtesy of David R. Harman, Jr.*

Underside of vaporizer lid.

Underside of vaporizer base.

Plate 539

Plate 540

Plate 541

Plate 542

Plate 540
Vase, 7"h., by John Tams & Son, England, c. 1913+, termed "moon vase" due to shape, pale blue underglaze, multicolored, beautiful, note the use of brown coloring for tree trunks and green for grass, gold trim on base over fish roe, $750.00 – 1,000.00+. *Courtesy of Loren Zeller.*

Plate 541
Vase, 12"h., paper label, Oriental Trading, brilliant white and blue colorings, modern, price in 1998, $20.00 – 35.00. *Courtesy of David R. Harman, Jr.*

Plate 542
Wall pocket, 6"h., unmarked, Japanese, standard (traditional) Willow pattern, hole for hanging, blue sponge-like border, $50.00 – 65.00. *Author's Collection.*

Plate 543

Warmer, candle insert, carafe sits atop warmer to keep the contents warm, unmarked, Japanese, $25.00 – 45.00. *Author's Collection.*

Plate 544

Watering pitcher, modern, for decorative use only, $35.00 – 50.00. *Author's Collection.*

Plate 545

Wash pitcher and basin, marked 1924 JAPAN, see Mark 97, $95.00 – 125.00. *Author's Collection.*

Plate 546

Wash pitcher and basin, unmarked, English, standard (traditional) Willow center pattern on pitcher and bowl, fancy molded rims with cobalt blue borders, $575.00 – 625.00 set. *Courtesy of David R. Harman, Jr.*

Plate 543

Plate 544

Plate 545

Plate 546

Plate 547

Plate 547

Wash pitcher and basin, Ye Old Blue Willow, English, see Mark 79, standard (traditional) Willow pattern and border, Willow motifs on outside of basin, beautiful, $575.00 – 650.00 set. *Courtesy of David R. Harman, Jr.*

Plate 548

Wash pitcher and basin, unmarked, English, Two Temples II pattern, parrott decal, no border, pale yellow, pitcher has two slots which might indicate a lid, $750.00 – 950.00. *Courtesy of Pam S. Donahue.*

Plate 548

Mark 1
William Alsager Adderley
Longton, Staffordshire, England
c. 1876 – 1885

Mark 2
William Alsager Adderley
Longton, Staffordshire, England
c. 1876 – 1885

Mark 3
William Adams & Sons
Longton, Staffordshire, England
c. 1893 – 1917

Mark 3
William Adams & Sons
Tunstall and Stoke, England
c. 1893 – 1917

Mark 4
Charles Allerton & Sons
Longton, Staffordshire, England
c. 1929 – 1942

Mark 5
Charles Allerton & Sons
Longton, Staffordshire, England
c. 1903 – 1912

Mark 5
Charles Allerton & Sons
Longton, Staffordshire, England
c. 1903 – 1912

Mark 5
Charles Allerton & Sons
Longton, Staffordshire, England
c. 1903 – 1912

Mark 6
G.L. Ashworth & Bros.
Fenton, England
twentieth century

Mark 7
G.L. Ashworth & Bros.
Hanley, Staffordshire, England
c. 1880+

Mark 7
G.L. Ashworth & Bros.
c. 1880+

Mark 7
G.L. Ashworth & Bros.
c. 1880+

Mark 8
Barker Bros. Ltd.
Longton, Staffordshire, England
c. 1930 – 1937

Mark 8
Barker Bros. Ltd.
c. 1930 – 1937

Mark 9
Frank Beardmore & Co.
Fenton, England
c. 1903 – 1914

Mark 10
Brown & Steventon Ltd.
Burslem, Staffordshire, England
Earthenware
c. 1903 – 1923

Mark 10
Brown & Steventon Ltd.
c. 1903 – 1923

Mark 10
Brown & Steventon Ltd.
c. 1903 – 1923

Mark 11
Booths
Tunstall, Staffordshire, England
c. 1906+

Mark 12a
Booths
c. 1912+

Mark 12b
Booths
c. 1912+

Mark 12c
Booths
c. 1912+

Mark 13
Bourne & Leigh
c. 1892 – 1939

Mark 13
Bourne & Leigh
c. 1892 – 1939

Mark 13
Bourne & Leigh
Burslem, Staffordshire, England
c. 1892 – 1939

Mark 13
Bourne & Leigh
c. 1892 – 1939

Mark 13
Bourne & Leigh
c. 1892 – 1939

Mark 14
Burgess & Leigh
c. 1930s+

Mark 14
Burgess & Leigh
c. 1930s+

Mark 15
Thomas Cone Ltd.
Longton, Staffordshire, England
c. 1946+

Mark 16
W.T. Copeland
Stoke, England
c. 1904 – 1954
(impressed 1927)

Mark 17
W.T. Copeland
Stoke, England
(double mark – John Ford)

Mark 18
W.T. Copeland for Tiffany, NY
Stoke, England
c. 1883+

Mark 19
Crown Staffordshire Porcelain Co. Ltd.
Fenton, Staffordshire, England
c. 1906 – 1930+

Mark 20
Churchill
Modern

Mark 21
J. Dimmock & Co.
Hanley, Staffordshire, England
c. 1862 – 1878

Mark 22
Doulton & Co., Ltd.
c. 1891 – 1902

Mark 22
Doulton & Co., Ltd.
Burslem, Staffordshire & Lambeth,
England
c. 1891 – 1902

Mark 23
Davenport
Longport, Staffordshire, England
c. 1870 – 1886

Mark 24
Royal Doulton
c. 1902 – 1930
(without "Made In England")
("Made In England," after 1930)

Mark 25
Edge, Malkin & Co.
Burslem, Staffordshire, England
c. 1873 – 1903

Mark 26
Gibson & Sons, Ltd.
Burslem, Staffordshire, England
c. 1912+

Mark 27
Globe Pottery Co. Ltd.
Cobridge, Staffordshire, England
c. 1917+

Mark 28
Grimwades Ltd.
Stoke, Staffordshire, England
(UHP stands for
Upper Hanley Pottery)

Mark 29
Grimwades Ltd.
Stoke, Staffordshire, England
c. 1951+

Mark 30
W.H. Grindley
Tunstall, Staffordshire, England
c. 1908+

Mark 31
Hillchurch Pottery
late twentieth century

Mark 32
George Jones & Sons
Stoke, Staffordshire, England
c. 1924 – 1951

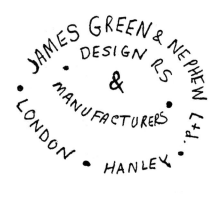

Mark 33
James Green & Nephew Ltd.

Mark 34
Old Hall Earthenware Co. Ltd.
c. 1861 – 1886

Mark 35
Old Hall Porcelain Works Ltd.
c. 1884 – 1902

Mark 36
Johnson Bros.
Hanley, Staffordshire, England
late twentieth century

Mark 37
Johnson Bros.
Hanley, Staffordshire, England
after 1912

Mark 38
J. Kent Ltd.
Longton, Staffordshire, England
c. 1913+

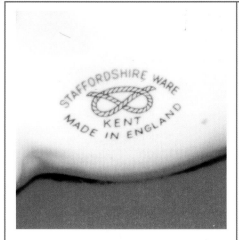

Mark 39
William Kent Ltd.
c. 1944 – 1962

Mark 40
Staffordshire Knot
William Kent Ltd.
Burslem, England
c. 1944 – 1962

Mark 41
Lancaster & Sandlar Ltd.
Hanley, England
c. 1949+

Mark 42
unknown manufacturer
Made in England

Mark 42
unknown manufacturer
Made in England

Mark 42
unknown manufacturer
Made in England

Mark 42
unknown manufacturer
Made in England

Mark 43
John Maddock & Sons Ltd.
Burslem, Staffordshire, England
c. 1896+

Mark 44
John Maddock & Sons Ltd.
c. 1961

Mark 44a
John Maddock & Sons Ltd.
c. 1896+

Mark 45
C. J. Mason
Charles James
Lane Delph, Staffordshire, England
after 1891

Mark 46
Alfred Meakin
Tunstall, Staffordshire, England
c. 1930s

Mark 46
Alfred Meakin
c. 1930s

Mark 47
Alfred Meakin
c. 1930s

Mark 47
Alfred Meakin
c. 1930s

Mark 48
W.R. Midwinter
Burslem, Staffordshire, England
c. 1946

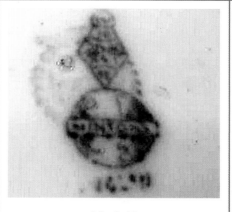

Mark 49
Mintons
Stoke, Staffordshire, England
c. 1873 – 1912
(the word "England" added after 1891)

Mark 50
Mintons
c. 1912 – 1950
(word "Willow" added)

Mark 51
Mintons
c. 1891 – 1902

Mark 52
New Hall Pottery Co. Ltd.
Hanley, Staffordshire, England
c. 1930 – 1951

Mark 53
Newport Pottery Company, Ltd.
Burslem, Staffordshire, England
c. 1920+

Mark 54
Simpsons
Colbridge, Staffordshire, England
c. 1944+

Mark 55
Regal
c. 1980s+

Mark 56
Ridgways
Hanley, Staffordshire, England
c. 1927

Mark 57
Ridgways
c. 1927

Mark 58
Ridgways
Bow and Quiver mark
alone with "England"
c. 1912 – 1927

Mark 59
Ridgways
("Made in Great Britain" added)
c. 1927

Mark 60
Ridgways
c. 1891+

Mark 61
possibly Ridgways
c. 1927+

Mark 62
Royal Worcester Porcelain Co.
Worcester, England
c. 1881

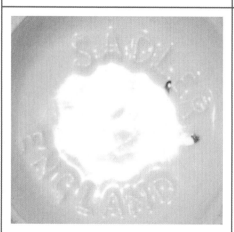

Mark 63
James Sadler & Sons
Burslem, Staffordshire, England
c. 1947

Mark 64
James Sadler & Sons
after 1947

Mark 64
James Sadler & Sons
after 1947

Mark 65
John Steventon & Sons, Ltd.
Burslem, Staffordshire, England
c. 1923 – 1936

Mark 66
John Steventon & Sons, Ltd.
c. 1923 – 1936

Mark 67
Swan Brand,
England
c. 1970s

Mark 68
Tuscan China
date unknown

Mark 69
Heath Wade & Co. Ltd.
Burslem & Stoke
Staffordshire, England
c. 1927+

Mark 70
Wedgwood & Co.
Tunstall, Staffordshire, England
c. 1891 – 1900

Mark 71
Wedgwood & Co.
c. 1906

Mark 71
Wedgwood & Co.
c. 1906

Mark 72
Josiah Wedgwood
Burslem, Etruria, & Barlaston
Staffordshire, England
c. 1891 – 1950

Mark 73
Wedgwood
c. 1900+
(words "England" or
"Made In England"
were added after 1891)

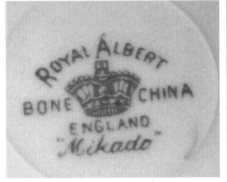

Mark 74
Thomas C. Wild & Sons
(Royal Albert Ltd.)
(now Royal Doulton Tableware Ltd.)
Longton, Staffordshire, England
c. 1917 – present

Mark 74a
Arthur Wood
Longport & Stoke
Staffordshire, England
c. 1904 – present

Mark 75
Wood & Sons, Ltd.
c. 1917+

Mark 75
Wood & Sons, Ltd.
c. 1917+

Mark 75
Wood & Sons, Ltd.
Burslem, Staffordshire, England
c. 1917+

Mark 75
Wood & Sons, Ltd.
c. 1917+

Mark 76
Wood & Sons, Ltd.
c. 1917 – 1930

Mark 77
Wood & Sons
c. 1818 – 1846

Mark 78
unknown English manufacturer

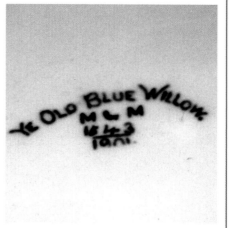

Mark 79
unknown English manufacturer

Mark 80
unknown English manufacturer
"Barrett Porcelain, England"

Mark 81
unknown English manufacturer
"Made In England for
L. Bamberger & Co."

Mark 82
Gold Castle
Made in Japan

Mark 83
Grant Crest
Japan

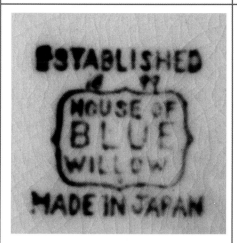

Mark 84
House of Blue Willow
Made in Japan

Mark 85
Made in Japan, Noritake
c. 1918 – 1941

Mark 86
JAPAN
twentieth century

Mark 87
"Nico"
Made in Japan
twentieth century

Mark 88
Wako China
Japan
twentieth century

Mark 89
Mandarin Blue
Maurta
c. 1940s – 1950s
JAPAN
unknown twentieth century manufacturer

Mark 90
JAPAN
unknown twentieth century manufacturer

Mark 92
JAPAN
unknown twentieth century manufacturer

Mark 95
Moriyama, Japan
c. 1945 – 1952

Mark 96
Nihon Koshitsu Toki Company
Ironstone Ware
Craftsman China
188 Willow Japan

Mark 97
JAPAN
1924

Mark 98
Made in Japan (black)

Mark 100
wreath mark
Made in Japan
twentieth century

Mark 101
Buffalo China Company
Buffalo, New York, USA
after 1915

Mark 99
Made in Japan (blue)

Mark 102
Buffalo Pottery
1908

Mark 103
Buffalo Pottery
1910

Mark 104
Buffalo Pottery
1911

Mark 105
Buffalo Pottery
1914

Mark 106
Buffalo Pottery Company
1916

Mark 107
Buffalo Pottery
c. 1905 – 1915

Mark 108
Cannonsburg Pottery Co.
Cannonsburg, Pennsylvania
c. 1901 – 1978

Mark 109
Flintridge China Company
Pasadena, California
c. 1945 – 1970

Mark 110
The George S. Thompson Corporation
Los Angeles, Monterey Park, & South
Pasadena, California

Mark 111
W.S. George Pottery Company
East Palestine, Ohio
c. late 1930s – late 1940s

Mark 112
Jackson China Company
Falls Creek, Pennsylvania, USA
c. 1951

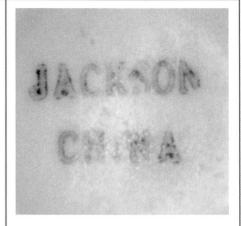

Mark 112
Jackson China Company
Falls Creek, Pennsylvania, USA
c. 1951

Mark 113
Jackson China Company
(Cook's Hotel & Restaurant
Supply Co. Inc.)
Falls Creek, Pennsylvania, USA

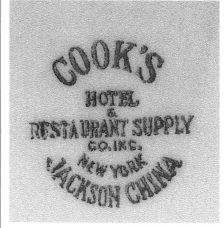

Mark 114
Jackson China Company
Falls Creek, Pennsylvania, USA

Mark 115
Homer Laughlin China Company
East Liverpool, Ohio,
and Newell, West Virginia
1944

Mark 116
Homer Laughlin China Compnay
East Liverpool, Ohio, and Newell,
West Virginia
c. 1930s – 1960s

Mark 117
Ideal
unknown manufacturer

Mark 118
Nelson McCoy Pottery
Roseville, Ohio
1910 – 1990

Mark 119
The Paden City Pottery Company
Paden City, West Virginia
c. 1914 – 1963

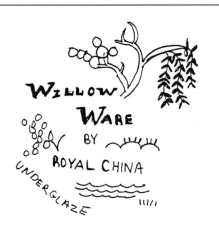

Mark 120
The Royal China Company
Sebring, Ohio
c. 1949 – 1960

Mark 121
The Royal China Company
Sebring, Ohio
c. 1934 – 1960

Mark 122
The Royal China Company
Sebring, Ohio
c. 1949 – 1960

Mark 123
Shenango China Company
New Castle, Pennsylvania
after 1948

Mark 124
Shenango China Company
New Castle, Pennsylvania
after 1948

Mark 125
Shenango China Company
New Castle, Pennsylvania

Mark 125a
Shenango China Company
New Castle, Pennsylvania
c. 1950s

Mark 125b
Shenango China Company
New Castle, Pennsylvania
c. 1950s

Mark 125c
Shenango China Company
New Castle, Pennsylvania
c. 1950s

Mark 125d
Shenango China Company
New Castle, Pennsylvania
c. 1950s

Mark 125e
Shenango China Company
New Castle, Pennsylvania
c. 1950s

Mark 126
Sterling China Company
Wellsville, Ohio
c. 1950s

Mark 127
Walker China Company
Bedford, Ohio
c. 1969

Mark 127a
Walker China Company
Bedford, Ohio
c. 1969

Mark 128
Hazel Atlas Glass Company
Clarksburg, West Virginia
c. 1902 – 1956

Mark 129
Brazil
"Germer, Porcelianas"
twentieth century

Mark 130
Made in China
designed in England
twentieth century

Mark 131
Gien
France
(impressed)

Mark 132
France
"Saneggemines"
with the initials "D.V."

Mark 133
A Royal Doulton Product
Made in Indonesia

Mark 134
Germany
Villeroy & Boch
Saar Basin
twentieth century

Mark 135
Petrus Regot
Maestricht, Holland
before 1891

Mark 136
Societe Ceramique
Maestricht, Holland
after 1891

Mark 137
Puerto Rico, USA

Mark 138
Sweden, Old Gustavsberg

Mark 139
unknown twentieth century manufacturer

Mark 140
Britanna Pottery Co., Ltd.
Glasgow, Scotland
c. 1920 – 1935

WILLOW PATTERN TEA HOUSE, NATIVE CITY.

Booths Ad
Blue Willow ad from the 1950s era featuring Booths pattern. Although no value can be placed on the ads, they are desired by collectors.

Postcard
Tea house resembling the pagoda often seen on the Willow pattern. Such tea houses may have been inspirations to the creators of the Willow pattern.

Basaltine Willow – term associated with the ware of Frank Beardmore & Co., Fenton, England, 1903 – 1914; the ware have a basalt-like finish. A basalt body has an unglazed matte surface. Also known as "Egyptian black."

Bisque Firing – the first firing or baking.

Bisque Ware – also called biscuit ware, unglazed clay ware, fired once.

Bone China – porcelain that contains bone ash which gives the appearance of added translucency, whiteness, and hardness.

Blue and White – porcelain and pottery ware around the eighteenth century decorated in underglaze blue, most likely in Oriental designs or landscapes.

Cobalt – element found in various ores such as copper, manganese, and iron that yields a deep blue color; an important color source.

Creamware – cream colored earthenware.

Crazing – tiny cracks in the glaze of the ceramic surface caused by the uneven contraction of the glaze and the body of the ware. Crazing might not appear right away; it may occur over time. Heat, moisture, and aging can cause crazing.

Decals – transferable decorative patterns which are applied either by low firing to allow them to melt onto the ware, wetting them and allowing them to adhere to the ware, or adhering pre-pasted decals that have a removable film (also called decalcomania).

Earthenware – this ware, when fired, is porous and opaque; clays and silica compounds are used to make earthenware.

Etching – patterns or marks that have been cut or carved into a ware (Depression glass and Cambridge ware, for example).

Finial – the knob on the top of a lid. Occasionally the finial will be a fancy or figural shape which resembles but is not limited to an animal, flower, or shape.

Flow Blue – a decoration used on hard, white bodied earthenware. The underglaze blue pattern is applied either by transfer printing or by hand brush strokes, then the ink is allowed to bleed or flow into the undecorated portions of the earthenware during firing. When lime or chloride of ammonia are added during a stage of firing the desired "flow" is achieved.

Flatware – flat or almost flat dinnerware, for example, plates or platters.

Gaudy Willow – vibrant hand-painted colors of greens, rust, cobalt, and pure gold coin on Willow pieces which enhance the underglaze printed brown with an overglaze. Buffalo Pottery & Ridgways called their multicolored ware "Gaudy Willow." (See Plate 329.)

Greenware – clay shapes that have not yet been fired.

Hollowware – items that are cast in molds, such as pitchers, gravy boats, casseroles, creamers, or sugars.

Impressed – marked or stamped by hand or in the mold by applying pressure.

Ironstone – a term not widely used today to describe a ware with a large iron content similar to stone china. This particular ware is enduring and strong, great for heavy items such as jugs and platters.

Jardiniere – an ornate flowerpot.

Moderntone Platonite – a heat resistant white glass that is a more solid white than opaque. (See Plate 379).

Multicolored – term used in this book to describe items that are decorated with more than one color. Synonymous with polychrome.

Nanking – a port in China. The term "nankin" was used by Staffordshire potters to describe certain inner borders and porcelain ornamentation. Robert Copeland's *Spode's Willow Pattern and Other Designs After the Chinese* elaborates on this term.

Opaque - if a ware is opaque, light cannot pass through it. Opacifier is material added to a transparent glaze to make it opaque.

Overglaze Decoration – applying color or other decorations to a ware after being fired. The heat of the kiln need not be as intense as at other stages, since the heat does not need to harden the glaze. You can easily identify overglaze by gliding your fingers over the ware. The change in the texture between the background and the decoration is overglaze.

Pearlware – white earthenware, similar to early creamware, but with more of a white appearance due to cobalt being added to the lead glaze.

Porcelain – vitreous, translucent ceramics. One should be able to see light through true porcelain.

Rubber Stamp Printing – the pattern would be created in the form of a rubber stamp, then stamped onto the ware before the glaze was applied. This method was simpler and less expensive for companies, but the quality of the images were sometimes not as clear as with transfer printing.

Stippling – a prime example of "stippling" can be found in some of the Royal Winton Pekin pattern backgrounds. The background appears to have the look of one taking the background color and repeatedly dabbing the color onto the ware, causing the background color to look like there are many round dots on it. (See Plate 248).

Temple-Landscape I Pattern – Chinese landscape pattern that most collectors consider Willow. Most distinguishing characteristics are the man carrying an umbrella on the bridge and the unusual inner border. The outer border varies with the Mandarin Temple-Landscape, true Fitzhugh with daggers and lattice work.

Transfer Printing – a design is etched into a metal (normally copper or steel) plate. The metal plate is then heated, and colored ink is applied and rubbed well into the etched plate. The excess color is removed, leaving the color that is worked into the design. The pattern is then transferred onto a tissue by going over it with a roller.

Translucent – ware that has been fired so intensely that a fair amount of light is able to pass through it. Porcelain is a prime example.

Underglaze – the pattern or decoration is applied to the bisque before it is glazed. After that is complete, the potter applies a clear glaze, and the ware is fired again. High temperatures are needed to harden the glaze.

Vitrified – glass-like state. A special glaze is applied and the ware is fired at a high temperature until the ware and the glaze fuse together.

Ware – the end result of pottery. This term is used to describe either one piece or an entire line, in any stage of the pottery process.

Bibliography

Books

Altman, Seymour and Violet. *The Book of Buffalo Pottery.* Crown Publishing Inc., New York, NY: 1969.

Copeland, Robert. *Spode's Willow Pattern and Other Designs After the Chinese, Third Edition.* Studio Vista, A Cassell Imprint, London, WC2R 0BB: 1999.

Cunningham, Jo. *The Collector's Encyclopedia of American Dinnerware.* Collector Books, Paducah, KY: 1999.

Duke, Harvey. *Official Price Guide to Pottery and Porcelain, Eighth Edition.* House of Collectibles, New York, NY: 1995.

Florence, Gene. *The Collector's Encyclopedia of Occupied Japan Collectibles, Fifth Series.* Collector Books, Paducah, KY: 1994.

Gaston, Mary Frank. *Blue Willow, An Identification and Value Guide, Revised Second Edition.* Collector Books, Paducah, KY: 1996.

Godden, Geoffrey A. *Encyclopaedia of British Pottery and Porcelain Marks.* Crown Publishers, New York, NY: 1964.

____. *Handbook of British Pottery and Porcelain Marks.* Barrie & Jenkins, London, England: 1974.

Johnson, Frances. *Kitchen Antiques.* Schiffer Publishing Ltd., Atglen, PA: 1996.

Kenny, John B. *The Complete Book of Pottery Making, Second Edition.* Chilton Book Company, Radnor, PA: 1976.

Kovel, Ralph and Terry. *Kovels' New Dictionary of Marks, 1850 – Present.* Crown Publishers, Inc., New York, NY: 1986.

Kowalsky, Arnold A. and Dorothy E. *Encyclopedia of Marks, 1780 – 1980.* Schiffer Publishing, Ltd., Atglen, PA: 1999.

Lehner, Lois. *Lehner's Encyclopedia of U.S. Marks on Pottery, Porcelain, & Clay.* Collector Books, Paducah, KY: 1988.

Lindbeck, Jennifer A. *A Collector's Guide to Willow Ware.* Schiffer Publishing, Ltd., Atglen, PA: 2000.

Rogers, Connie. *Willow Ware Made in the U.S.A. Identification Guide.* Self published, Cincinnati, OH: 1995.

Schroeder's Antiques Price Guide, Fourteenth Edition. Collector Books, Paducah, KY: 1996.

Snyder, Jeff B. *Flow Blue: A Collector's Guide to Pattern, History, and Values.* Schiffer Publishing, Ltd., Atglen, PA: 1994.

Worth, Veryl Marie and Louise M. Loehr. *Willow Pattern China, Fourth Edition.* H.S. Worth Co., Kutztown, PA: 1991. Distributed by Louise's Old Things, Kutztown, PA.

Newsletters/Catalogs

International Willow Collectors annual convention catalogs, Volume II, 1994, Volume VIII, 2000. Membership information: 503 Chestnut Street, Perkasie, PA 18944. Website Address: www.willowcollectors.org

Willow Word Newsletter, Volume 9, No. 3-6, Volume 10, No. 2-6, Volume 11, Nos. 1, 5, 6. Mary Lina Berndt, publisher (now known as the *Willow Review*).

Willow Review Newsletter, The Newsletter for Willow Enthusiasts around the World, publisher and editor Jeff W. Siptak, Volume 2, Numbers 2-4. Ordering information: The Willow Review, P.O. Box 41312, Nashville, TN 37204-1312, e-mail address: willowware@aol.com

Willow Patterns Index

— *Willow Patterns Index* —

Willow Manufacturers Index

— *Willow Manufacturers Index* —

COLLECTOR BOOKS

Informing Today's Collector

For over two decades we have been keeping collectors informed on trends and values in all fields of antiques and collectibles.

DOLLS, FIGURES & TEDDY BEARS

4707	A Decade of **Barbie Dolls** & Collectibles, 1981–1991, Summers	$19.95
4631	**Barbie Doll** Boom, 1986–1995, Augustyniak	$18.95
2079	**Barbie Doll** Fashion, Volume I, Eames	$24.95
4846	**Barbie Doll** Fashion, Volume II, Eames	$24.95
3957	**Barbie** Exclusives, Rana	$18.95
4632	**Barbie** Exclusives, Book II, Rana	$18.95
5672	The **Barbie Doll** Years, 4th Ed., Olds	$19.95
3810	**Chatty Cathy** Dolls, Lewis	$15.95
5352	Collector's Ency. of **Barbie** Doll Exclusives & More, 2nd Ed.,Augustyniak	$24.95
2211	Collector's Encyclopedia of **Madame Alexander** Dolls, Smith	$24.95
4863	Collector's Encyclopedia of **Vogue Dolls**, Izen/Stover	$29.95
5821	**Doll Values**, Antique to Modern, 5th Ed., Moyer	$12.95
5829	**Madame Alexander** Collector's Dolls Price Guide #26, Crowsey	$12.95
5833	**Modern Collectible Dolls**, Volume V, Moyer	$24.95
5689	**Nippon Dolls** & Playthings, Van Patten/Lau	$29.95
5365	**Peanuts Collectibles**, Podley/Bang	$24.95
5253	Story of **Barbie**, 2nd Ed., Westenhouser	$24.95
5277	**Talking Toys** of the 20th Century, Lewis	$15.95
1513	**Teddy Bears & Steiff** Animals, Mandel	$9.95
1817	**Teddy Bears & Steiff** Animals, 2nd Series, Mandel	$19.95
2084	**Teddy Bears, Annalee's & Steiff** Animals, 3rd Series, Mandel	$19.95
5371	**Teddy Bear** Treasury, Yenke	$19.95
1808	Wonder of **Barbie**, Manos	$9.95
1430	World of **Barbie** Dolls, Manos	$9.95
4880	World of **Raggedy Ann** Collectibles, Avery	$24.95

TOYS, MARBLES & CHRISTMAS COLLECTIBLES

2333	Antique & Collectible **Marbles**, 3rd Ed., Grist	$9.95
5353	**Breyer Animal** Collector's Guide, 2nd Ed., Browell	$19.95
4976	**Christmas Ornaments**, Lights & Decorations, Johnson	$24.95
4737	**Christmas Ornaments**, Lights & Decorations, Vol. II, Johnson	$24.95
4739	**Christmas Ornaments**, Lights & Decorations, Vol. III, Johnson	$24.95
4559	Collectible **Action Figures**, 2nd Ed., Manos	$17.95
2338	Collector's Encyclopedia of **Disneyana**, Longest, Stern	$24.95
5038	Collector's Guide to **Diecast Toys** & Scale Models, 2nd Ed., Johnson	$19.95
4651	Collector's Guide to **Tinker Toys**, Strange	$18.95
4566	Collector's Guide to **Tootsietoys**, 2nd Ed., Richter	$19.95
5169	Collector's Guide to **TV Toys** & Memorabilia, 2nd Ed., Davis/Morgan	$24.95
5360	**Fisher-Price Toys**, Cassity	$19.95
4720	The Golden Age of **Automotive Toys**, 1925–1941, Hutchison/Johnson	$24.95
5593	Grist's Big Book of **Marbles**, 2nd Ed.	$24.95
3970	Grist's Machine-Made & Contemporary **Marbles**, 2nd Ed.	$9.95
5267	**Matchbox Toys**, 1947 to 1998, 3rd Ed., Johnson	$19.95
5830	**McDonald's** Collectibles, 2nd Edition, Henriques/DuVall	$24.95
5673	Modern **Candy Containers** & Novelties, Brush/Miller	$19.95
1540	Modern **Toys** 1930–1980, Baker	$19.95
3888	**Motorcycle Toys**, Antique & Contemporary, Gentry/Downs	$18.95
5693	**Schroeder's Collectible Toys**, Antique to Modern Price Guide, 7th Ed.	$17.95

FURNITURE

1457	American **Oak** Furniture, McNerney	$9.95
3716	American **Oak** Furniture, Book II, McNerney	$12.95
1118	Antique **Oak** Furniture, Hill	$7.95
2271	Collector's Encyclopedia of **American** Furniture, Vol. II, Swedberg	$24.95
3720	Collector's Encyclopedia of **American** Furniture, Vol. III, Swedberg	$24.95
5359	Early **American** Furniture, Obbard	$12.95
1755	Furniture of the **Depression Era**, Swedberg	$19.95
3906	**Heywood-Wakefield** Modern Furniture, Rouland	$18.95
1885	**Victorian** Furniture, Our American Heritage, McNerney	$9.95
3829	**Victorian** Furniture, Our American Heritage, Book II, McNerney	$9.95

JEWELRY, HATPINS, WATCHES & PURSES

1712	Antique & Collectible **Thimbles** & Accessories, Mathis	$19.95
1748	Antique **Purses**, Revised Second Ed., Holiner	$19.95
1278	Art Nouveau & Art Deco **Jewelry**, Baker	$9.95
4850	Collectible **Costume Jewelry**, Simonds	$24.95
5675	Collectible **Silver Jewelry**, Rezazadeh	$24.95
3722	Collector's Ency. of **Compacts**, Carryalls & Face Powder Boxes, Mueller	$24.95
4940	**Costume Jewelry**, A Practical Handbook & Value Guide, Rezazadeh	$24.95
1716	Fifty Years of Collectible **Fashion Jewelry**, 1925–1975, Baker	$19.95
1424	**Hatpins** & Hatpin Holders, Baker	$9.95
5695	**Ladies' Vintage Accessories**, Bruton	$24.95
1181	100 Years of Collectible **Jewelry**, 1850–1950, Baker	$9.95
4729	**Sewing Tools** & Trinkets, Thompson	$24.95
5620	Unsigned Beauties of **Costume Jewelry**, Brown	$24.95
4878	Vintage & Contemporary **Purse Accessories**, Gerson	$24.95
5696	Vintage & Vogue Ladies' **Compacts**, 2nd Edition, Gerson	$29.95

INDIANS, GUNS, KNIVES, TOOLS, PRIMITIVES

1868	Antique **Tools**, Our American Heritage, McNerney	$9.95
5616	Big Book of **Pocket Knives**, Stewart	$19.95
4943	Field Guide to Flint **Arrowheads & Knives** of the North American Indian	$9.95
2279	**Indian Artifacts** of the Midwest, Book I, Hothem	$14.95
3885	**Indian Artifacts** of the Midwest, Book II, Hothem	$16.95
4870	**Indian Artifacts** of the Midwest, Book III, Hothem	$18.95
5685	**Indian Artifacts** of the Midwest, Book IV, Hothem	$19.95
5687	**Modern Guns**, Identification & Values, 13th Ed., Quertermous	$14.95
2164	**Primitives**, Our American Heritage, McNerney	$9.95
1759	**Primitives**, Our American Heritage, 2nd Series, McNerney	$14.95
4730	Standard **Knife** Collector's Guide, 3rd Ed., Ritchie & Stewart	$12.95

PAPER COLLECTIBLES & BOOKS

4633	**Big Little Books**, Jacobs	$18.95
4710	Collector's Guide to **Children's Books**, 1850 to 1950, Volume I, Jones	$18.95
5153	Collector's Guide to **Chldren's Books**, 1850 to 1950, Volume II, Jones	$19.95
5596	Collector's Guide to **Children's Books**, 1950 to 1975, Volume III, Jones	$19.95
1441	Collector's Guide to **Post Cards**, Wood	$9.95
2081	Guide to Collecting **Cookbooks**, Allen	$14.95
5825	Huxford's **Old Book** Value Guide, 13th Ed.	$19.95
2080	Price Guide to **Cookbooks** & Recipe Leaflets, Dickinson	$9.95
3973	**Sheet Music** Reference & Price Guide, 2nd Ed., Pafik & Guiheen	$19.95
4654	**Victorian Trade Cards**, Historical Reference & Value Guide, Cheadle	$19.95
4733	**Whitman Juvenile Books**, Brown	$17.95

GLASSWARE

5602	Anchor Hocking's **Fire-King** & More, 2nd Ed.	$24.95
4561	Collectible **Drinking Glasses**, Chase & Kelly	$17.95
5823	Collectible **Glass Shoes**, 2nd Edition, Wheatley	$24.95
5357	Coll. **Glassware** from the 40s, 50s & 60s, 5th Ed., Florence	$19.95
1810	Collector's Encyclopedia of **American Art Glass**, Shuman	$29.95
5358	Collector's Encyclopedia of **Depression Glass**, 14th Ed., Florence	$19.95
1961	Collector's Encyclopedia of **Fry Glassware**, Fry Glass Society	$24.95
1664	Collector's Encyclopedia of **Heisey Glass**, 1925–1938, Bredehoft	$24.95
3905	Collector's Encyclopedia of **Milk Glass**, Newbound	$24.95
4936	Collector's Guide to **Candy Containers**, Dezso/Poirier	$19.95
4564	**Crackle Glass**, Weitman	$19.95
4941	**Crackle Glass**, Book II, Weitman	$19.95
4714	**Czechoslovakian Glass** and Collectibles, Book II, Barta/Rose	$16.95
5528	Early American **Pattern Glass**, Metz	$17.95
5682	**Elegant Glassware** of the Depression Era, 9th Ed., Florence	$19.95
5614	Field Guide to **Pattern Glass**, McCain	$17.95
3981	Evers' Standard **Cut Glass** Value Guide	$12.95
4659	**Fenton** Art Glass, 1907–1939, Whitmyer	$24.95
5615	Florence's **Glassware Pattern Identification** Guide, Vol. II	$19.95

COLLECTOR BOOKS
Informing Today's Collector

4719	**Fostoria**, Etched, Carved & Cut Designs, Vol. II, Kerr	$24.95
3883	**Fostoria Stemware**, The Crystal for America, Long/Seate	$24.95
5261	**Fostoria Tableware**, 1924 – 1943, Long/Seate	$24.95
5361	**Fostoria Tableware**, 1944 – 1986, Long/Seate	$24.95
5604	**Fostoria**, Useful & Ornamental, Long/Seate	$29.95
4644	**Imperial Carnival Glass**, Burns	$18.95
5827	**Kitchen Glassware** of the Depression Years, 6th Ed., Florence	$24.95
5600	Much More Early American **Pattern Glass**, Metz	$17.95
5690	Pocket Guide to **Depression Glass**, 12th Ed., Florence	$9.95
5594	Standard Encyclopedia of **Carnival Glass**, 7th Ed., Edwards/Carwile	$29.95
5595	Standard **Carnival Glass** Price Guide, 12th Ed., Edwards/Carwile	$9.95
5272	Standard Encyclopedia of **Opalescent Glass**, 3rd Ed., Edwards/Carwile	$24.95
5617	Standard Encyclopedia of **Pressed Glass**, 2nd Ed., Edwards/Carwile	$29.95
4731	**Stemware Identification**, Featuring Cordials with Values, Florence	$24.95
4732	**Very Rare Glassware** of the Depression Years, 5th Series, Florence	$24.95
4656	**Westmoreland Glass**, Wilson	$24.95

POTTERY

4927	**ABC Plates & Mugs**, Lindsay	$24.95
4929	**American Art Pottery**, Sigafoose	$24.95
4630	**American Limoges**, Limoges	$24.95
1312	**Blue & White Stoneware**, McNerney	$9.95
1958	So. Potteries **Blue Ridge Dinnerware**, 3rd Ed., Newbound	$14.95
1959	**Blue Willow**, 2nd Ed., Gaston	$14.95
4851	Collectible **Cups & Saucers**, Harran	$18.95
1373	Collector's Encyclopedia of **American Dinnerware**, Cunningham	$24.95
4931	Collector's Encyclopedia of **Bauer Pottery**, Chipman	$24.95
4932	Collector's Encyclopedia of **Blue Ridge Dinnerware**, Vol. II, Newbound	$24.95
4658	Collector's Encyclopedia of **Brush-McCoy Pottery**, Huxford	$24.95
5034	Collector's Encyclopedia of **California Pottery**, 2nd Ed., Chipman	$24.95
2133	Collector's Encyclopedia of **Cookie Jars**, Roerig	$24.95
3723	Collector's Encyclopedia of **Cookie Jars**, Book II, Roerig	$24.95
4939	Collector's Encyclopedia of **Cookie Jars**, Book III, Roerig	$24.95
5748	Collector's Encyclopedia of **Fiesta**, 9th Ed., Huxford	$24.95
4718	Collector's Encyclopedia of **Figural Planters & Vases**, Newbound	$19.95
3961	Collector's Encyclopedia of **Early Noritake**, Alden	$24.95
1439	Collector's Encyclopedia of **Flow Blue China**, Gaston	$19.95
3812	Collector's Encyclopedia of **Flow Blue China**, 2nd Ed., Gaston	$24.95
3431	Collector's Encyclopedia of **Homer Laughlin China**, Jasper	$24.95
1276	Collector's Encyclopedia of **Hull Pottery**, Roberts	$19.95
3962	Collector's Encyclopedia of **Lefton China**, DeLozier	$19.95
4855	Collector's Encyclopedia of **Lefton China**, Book II, DeLozier	$19.95
5609	Collector's Encyclopedia of **Limoges Porcelain**, 3rd Ed., Gaston	$29.95
2334	Collector's Encyclopedia of **Majolica Pottery**, Katz-Marks	$19.95
1358	Collector's Encyclopedia of **McCoy Pottery**, Huxford	$19.95
5677	Collector's Encyclopedia of **Niloak**, 2nd Edition, Gifford	$29.95
3837	Collector's Encyclopedia of **Nippon Porcelain**, Van Patten	$24.95
1665	Collector's Ency. of **Nippon Porcelain**, 3rd Series, Van Patten	$24.95
4712	Collector's Ency. of **Nippon Porcelain**, 4th Series, Van Patten	$24.95
5053	Collector's Ency. of **Nippon Porcelain**, 5th Series, Van Patten	$24.95
5678	Collector's Ency. of **Nippon Porcelain**, 6th Series, Van Patten	$29.95
1447	Collector's Encyclopedia of **Noritake**, Van Patten	$19.95
1038	Collector's Encyclopedia of **Occupied Japan**, 2nd Series, Florence	$14.95
4951	Collector's Encyclopedia of **Old Ivory China**, Hillman	$24.95
5564	Collector's Encyclopedia of **Pickard China**, Reed	$29.95
3877	Collector's Encyclopedia of **R.S. Prussia**, 4th Series, Gaston	$24.95
5679	Collector's Encyclopedia of **Red Wing Art Pottery**, Dollen	$24.95
5618	Collector's Encyclopedia of **Rosemeade Pottery**, Dommel	$24.95
5841	Collector's Encyclopedia of **Roseville Pottery**, Revised, Huxford/Nickel	$24.95
5842	Collector's Encyclopedia of **Roseville Pottery**, 2nd Series, Huxford/Nickel	$24.95
4713	Collector's Encyclopedia of **Salt Glaze Stoneware**, Taylor/Lowrance	$24.95
3314	Collector's Encyclopedia of **Van Briggle Art Pottery**, Sasicki	$24.95
4563	Collector's Encyclopedia of **Wall Pockets**, Newbound	$19.95
2111	Collector's Encyclopedia of **Weller Pottery**, Huxford	$29.95
5680	Collector's Guide to **Feather Edge Ware**, McAllister	$19.95
3876	Collector's Guide to **Lu-Ray Pastels**, Meehan	$18.95

3814	Collector's Guide to **Made in Japan Ceramics**, White	$18.95
4646	Collector's Guide to **Made in Japan Ceramics**, Book II, White	$18.95
2339	Collector's Guide to **Shawnee Pottery**, Vanderbilt	$19.95
1425	**Cookie Jars**, Westfall	$9.95
3440	**Cookie Jars**, Book II, Westfall	$19.95
4924	Figural & Novelty **Salt & Pepper Shakers**, 2nd Series, Davern	$24.95
2379	Lehner's Ency. of **U.S. Marks** on Pottery, Porcelain & China	$24.95
4722	**McCoy Pottery**, Collector's Reference & Value Guide, Hanson/Nissen	$19.95
5691	**Post86 Fiesta**, Identification & Value Guide, Racheter	$19.95
1670	**Red Wing Collectibles**, DePasquale	$9.95
1440	**Red Wing Stoneware**, DePasquale	$9.95
1632	**Salt & Pepper Shakers**, Guarnaccia	$9.95
5091	**Salt & Pepper Shakers** II, Guarnaccia	$18.95
3443	**Salt & Pepper Shakers** IV, Guarnaccia	$18.95
3738	**Shawnee Pottery**, Mangus	$24.95
4629	Turn of the Century **American Dinnerware**, 1880s–1920s, Jasper	$24.95
3327	**Watt Pottery** – Identification & Value Guide, Morris	$19.95

OTHER COLLECTIBLES

5838	Advertising **Thermometers**, Merritt	$16.95
4704	Antique & Collectible **Buttons**, Wisniewski	$19.95
2269	Antique **Brass & Copper** Collectibles, Gaston	$16.95
1880	Antique **Iron**, McNerney	$9.95
3872	Antique **Tins**, Dodge	$24.95
4845	Antique **Typewriters & Office Collectibles**, Rehr	$19.95
5607	Antiquing and Collecting on the **Internet**, Parry	$12.95
1128	**Bottle** Pricing Guide, 3rd Ed., Cleveland	$7.95
3718	Collectible **Aluminum**, Grist	$16.95
4560	Collectible **Cats**, An Identification & Value Guide, Book II, Fyke	$19.95
5060	Collectible **Souvenir Spoons**, Bednersh	$19.95
5676	Collectible **Souvenir Spoons**, Book II, Bednersh	$29.95
5666	Collector's Encyclopedia of **Granite Ware**, Book 2, Greguire	$29.95
5836	Collector's Guide to **Antique Radios**, 5th Ed., Bunis	$19.95
5608	Collector's Gde. to Buying, Selling & Trading on the **Internet**, 2nd Ed., Hix	$12.95
4637	Collector's Guide to **Cigarette Lighters**, Book II, Flanagan	$17.95
3966	Collector's Guide to **Inkwells**, Identification & Values, Badders	$18.95
4947	Collector's Guide to **Inkwells**, Book II, Badders	$19.95
5681	Collector's Guide to **Lunchboxes**, White	$19.95
5621	Collector's Guide to **Online Auctions**, Hix	$12.95
4862	Collector's Guide to **Toasters** & Accessories, Greguire	$19.95
4652	Collector's Guide to **Transistor Radios**, 2nd Ed., Bunis	$16.95
4864	Collector's Guide to **Wallace Nutting Pictures**, Ivankovich	$18.95
1629	**Doorstops**, Identification & Values, Bertoia	$9.95
5683	**Fishing Lure** Collectibles, 2nd Ed., Murphy/Edmisten	$29.95
5259	**Flea Market Trader**, 12th Ed., Huxford	$9.95
4945	**G-Men and FBI Toys** and Collectibles, Whitworth	$18.95
5605	**Garage Sale & Flea Market Annual**, 8th Ed.	$19.95
3819	**General Store** Collectibles, Wilson	$24.95
5159	Huxford's Collectible **Advertising**, 4th Ed.	$24.95
2216	**Kitchen Antiques**, 1790–1940, McNerney	$14.95
5686	**Lighting Fixtures** of the Depression Era, Book I, Thomas	$24.95
4950	The **Lone Ranger**, Collector's Reference & Value Guide, Felbinger	$18.95
2026	**Railroad** Collectibles, 4th Ed., Baker	$14.95
5619	**Roy Rogers and Dale Evans** Toys & Memorabilia, Coyle	$24.95
5692	**Schroeder's Antiques Price Guide**, 19th Ed., Huxford	$14.95
5007	**Silverplated Flatware**, Revised 4th Edition, Hagan	$18.95
5694	Summers' Guide to **Coca-Cola**, 3rd Ed.	$24.95
5356	Summers' Pocket Guide to **Coca-Cola**, 2nd Ed.	$9.95
3892	**Toy & Miniature Sewing Machines**, Thomas	$18.95
4876	**Toy & Miniature Sewing Machines**, Book II, Thomas	$24.95
5144	Value Guide to **Advertising Memorabilia**, 2nd Ed., Summers	$19.95
3977	Value Guide to **Gas Station Memorabilia**, Summers & Priddy	$24.95
4877	Vintage **Bar Ware**, Visakay	$24.95
4935	The W.F. Cody **Buffalo Bill** Collector's Guide with Values	$24.95
5281	**Wanted to Buy**, 7th Edition	$9.95

This is only a partial listing of the books on antiques that are available from Collector Books. All books are well illustrated and contain current values. Most of these books are available from your local bookseller, antique dealer, or public library. If you are unable to locate certain titles in your area, you may order by mail from COLLECTOR BOOKS, P.O. Box 3009, Paducah, KY 42002-3009. Customers with Visa, Discover or MasterCard may phone in orders from 7:00–5:00 CST, Monday–Friday, Toll Free 1-800-626-5420, or online at www.collectorbooks.com. Add $3.00 for postage for the first book ordered and 50¢ for each additional book. Include item number, title, and price when ordering. Allow 14 to 21 days for delivery.